Pocket French Grammar

Beginner, Intermediate, and Advanced Levels
Fifth Edition

by
Christopher Kendr
Diplômé, Faculté des Lettres
de Phonétique, Paris (en Sor

Certificat, École Pédagogique de l'Alliance Française de Paris
B.S., M.S., Columbia University in the City of New York
M.A., Ph.D., Northwestern University in Evanston, Illinois

Former Chairman
Department of Foreign Languages
Farmingdale High School
Farmingdale, New York

Theodore Kendris, Ph.D.
Ph.D., Université Laval, Québec, Canada
Former Instructor
Commonwealth University of Pennsylvania

To the memory of
Christopher and Yolanda Kendris
With love

Kaplan North America, LLC d/b/a Barron's Educational Series
1515 West Cypress Creek Road
Fort Lauderdale, Florida 33309
www.barronseduc.com

ISBN: 978-1-5062-9570-1

10 9 8 7 6 5 4 3 2 1

Kaplan North America, LLC d/b/a Barron's Educational Series
print books are available at special quantity discounts to use
for sales promotions, employee premiums, or educational pur-
poses. For more information or to purchase books, please call
the Simon & Schuster special sales department at
866-506-1949.

Table of Contents

Special Topics

About the Authors

Dr. Christopher Kendris worked as an interpreter and translator of French for the U.S. State Department at the American Embassy in Paris. He earned his B.S. in the School of General Studies and his M.S. in the School of Library Service, both at Columbia University in the City of New York, where he held a New York State Scholarship. He earned his M.A. and Ph.D. at Northwestern University in Evanston, Illinois, where he held a teaching assistantship and tutorial fellowship for four years. He also earned two diplomas with *Mention très Honorable* at the Université de Paris (en Sorbonne), Faculté des Lettres, École Supérieure de Préparation et de Perfectionnement des Professeurs de Français à l'Étranger, and at the Institut de Phonétique, Paris.

In 1986, Dr. Kendris was one of ninety-five teachers in the United States to be awarded a Rockefeller Foundation Fellowship for Teachers of Foreign Languages in American High Schools. He had forty years of teaching experience. Dr. Kendris taught French and Spanish at the University of Chicago as a visiting summer lecturer, as well as at Colby College, Duke University, Rutgers (the State University of New Jersey), the State University of New York at Albany, the Albany Academy, the Schenectady School District, and the Schenectady County Community College in New York. He was Chairman of the Department of Foreign Languages at Farmingdale High School in Farmingdale, New York. Dr. Kendris was the author of thirty-two secondary school and college books, workbooks, and other language guides of French and Spanish, some of which have been best sellers since 1970 all over the world, and all of which have been published by Barron's Educational Series.

Dr. Theodore Kendris earned his B.A. in modern languages at Union College in Schenectady, New York, where he received the Thomas J. Judson Memorial Award for modern language study. He went on to earn his M.A. in French language and literature at Northwestern University in Evanston, Illinois, where he was a teaching assistant and senior teaching fellow. He earned his Ph.D. in French literature at l'Université Laval in Quebec City, where he studied the Middle Ages and Renaissance. While at Université Laval, he taught French writing skills as *chargé de cours* in the French as a Second Language program, and in 1997 he was awarded a doctoral scholarship by the Fondation de l'Université Laval. Dr. Kendris has also taught in the Department of English and Foreign Languages at the University of St. Francis in Joliet, Illinois, as well as at the Hazleton campus of Penn State University. He has most recently been an instructor at the Bloomsburg and Lock Haven campuses of the Commonwealth University of Pennsylvania.

Dr. Kendris is the author of *Inglés completo: Repaso integral de gramática inglesa para hispanohablantes, Segunda edición*, published by Barron's. He is also the coauthor of several language guides, including *Pronounce It Perfectly in French*, *French Vocabulary*, *E-Z French*, *501 Spanish Verbs*, and *501 French Verbs*, also published by Barron's.

How to Use This Book

In the chapters that follow, a numerical decimal system has been used with the symbol § in front of it. This was done so that you may find quickly and easily the reference to a particular point in basic French grammar when you use the index. For example, if you look up the entry "adjectives" in the index, you will find the reference given as §5. Sometimes additional § reference numbers are given when the entry you consult is mentioned in other areas in the chapter §. For example, in §5.3, there is an explanation of how to decide whether an adjective belongs before or after the noun that it modifies. The index also includes some key French words, for example, *avoir* and *être*, with § references also assigned to them.

Preface

This book is part of a series of handy basic grammar reference guides. It is designed for students, businesspeople, and others who want to "brush up" their knowledge of basic French grammar. Definitions and explanations are concise and clear. Plenty of examples use and reuse a core of basic vocabulary.

This pocket-size book contains essential French grammar that is normally in the curriculum of beginning, intermediate, and advanced language programs. It is a reference grammar review book of all three levels. We hope you enjoy, in particular, our section on what preposition goes with what verb, found on pages 69–81.

The complete grammar review consists of three parts: the Basics, the Parts of Speech, and Special Topics, all of which are outlined in the table of contents.

Here and there we offer some tips to help you remember certain aspects of French grammar and vocabulary. For example, if you cannot remember whether the French word for twenty (vingt) is spelled *ng* or *gn*, remember it this way:

Mnemonic tips are very useful in learning and remembering. Students learn and remember in different ways. What works for you may not work for someone else. You must think of ways to help yourself remember. If you think of a way that is helpful, let it work for you. One student in a Spanish class, for example, told Dr. C. Kendris that she finally figured out a way to remember the meaning of the Spanish verb *buscar* / to look for. She said, "I'm looking for a bus or a car." How many mnemonic tips can you make up in French? Try it. It's fun!

Here are a few more: If someone asks you, "What are the five major Romance Languages?" are you going to say you don't know? Remember **FRIPS**:

Tip	**F**rench
	Romanian
	Italian
	Portuguese
	Spanish

To remember that there are only four nasal vowels in French, hang on to this catchy phrase because each word contains one of the four nasal vowels:

Tip	*un bon vin blanc* / a good white wine

If you keep pronouncing *un œuf* / an egg incorrectly, say this out loud:

Tip	Do you want one egg? Two eggs?
	One egg is enough!
	One egg is *un œuf*!

The sound of the English word "enough" is very close to the sound of the French word *un œuf.*

There are more mnemonic tips throughout this book. If we have omitted anything you think is important, if you spot any misprints, or if you have any suggestions for the improvement of the next edition, please write to us, care of the publisher.

This edition of *French Grammar* contains numerous sample sentences and three fully conjugated regular verbs (§7.20) to help you see the conjugation patterns more clearly. The section number at the top of each page will help you find what you are looking for quickly and easily.

We hope that you will find this book useful as you improve your knowledge of French grammar.

Christopher Kendris and Theodore Kendris

The Basics, Beginner Level

§1.

Guide to Pronouncing French Sounds

English words given here contain sounds that only approximate French sounds. To account for various differences in pronunciation among English speakers, we have included the International Phonetic Alphabet (IPA) phonetic symbols for each of the sounds. You can find the IPA symbols inside brackets in the column to the right of the English word approximations.

	PURE VOWEL SOUNDS	
French word	**Pronounced as in the English word**	**IPA symbol**
la	lolly, Tom	[a]
pas	ah!	[ɑ]
été	ate	[e]
ère, tête	egg	[ɛ]
ici	see	[i]
hôtel	over	[o]
donne	bun, done	[ɔ]
ou	too	[u]

leur	**ur**gent (approx. sound)	[œ]
deux	p**u**dding (approx. sound)	[ø]
tu	c**u**te (approx. sound)	[y]
le	**a**go (approx. sound)	[ə]

NASAL VOWEL SOUNDS

(English sounds are approximate.)

un	**un**guent, s**u**ng	[œ̃]
bon	s**o**ng	[ɔ̃]
vin	s**a**ng	[ɛ̃]
blanc	thr**o**ng	[ɑ̃]

SEMICONSONANT SOUNDS

(Also called semivowels)

oui	**w**est	[w]
huit	y**ou ea**t (approx. sound)	[ɥ]
fille	**y**es, see **y**a later	[j]

CONSONANT SOUNDS

French word	Pronounced as in the English word	IPA symbol
bonne	**b**un	[b]

Before the letter **s,** the letter **b** is pronounced as a **p** in French: *absolument* [apsɔly' mɑ̃] / absolutely

dans	**d**og	[d]
fou	**f**irst, **ph**armacy	[f]
garçon	**g**o	[g]
je	mea**s**ure	[ʒ]
chose	**sh**ake	[ʃ]
café, qui	**c**ap, **k**ennel	[k]
le	**l**et	[l]
mette	**m**et	[m]
nette	**n**et	[n]

montagne	ca**ny**on, o**ni**on, u**ni**on	[ɲ]
camping	campi**ng**, sleepi**ng**	[ŋ]
père	**p**ear	[p]
rose	**r**ose (approx. sound; the French sound is pronounced further back in the throat.)	[r]
si	**s**ee	[s]
te	lo**t**	[t]
vous	**v**ine	[v]
zèbre	**z**ebra	[z]
ça	**s**orry	[s]

- If you can, give equal stress to all syllables in a French word; do not raise your voice on any particular syllable.
- If you can't give equal stress to all syllables in a French word, then raise your voice slightly on the last syllable.

  Examples:
  chapeau (shah-PO), *magazine* (mah-gah-ZEEN), *perspicacité* (per-spee-kah-see-TAY)

- Do not pronounce the last letter of a French word if it is a consonant.

  Examples:
  beaucoup (bo-KOO), *aéroport* (ah-air-o-POR)

Some common exceptions: *parc* (pARK), *chef* (shEFF), *avec* (ah-VEK), and *août* (**oot**), although you may sometimes hear the word pronounced as **oo**. If you're not sure, don't pronounce the last consonant at all.

Tip	If you don't know which is *accent aigu* (acute) (é) and which is *accent grave* (è), remember that the patient died of acute appendicitis (é) and ended up in the grave (è).

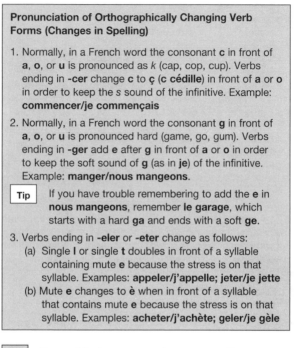

Pronunciation of Orthographically Changing Verb Forms (Changes in Spelling)

1. Normally, in a French word the consonant **c** in front of **a**, **o**, or **u** is pronounced as *k* (cap, cop, cup). Verbs ending in **-cer** change **c** to **ç** (**c cédille**) in front of **a** or **o** in order to keep the *s* sound of the infinitive. Example: **commencer/je commençais**

2. Normally, in a French word the consonant **g** in front of **a**, **o**, or **u** is pronounced hard (game, go, gum). Verbs ending in **-ger** add **e** after **g** in front of **a** or **o** in order to keep the soft sound of **g** (as in **je**) of the infinitive. Example: **manger/nous mangeons**.

   | Tip | If you have trouble remembering to add the **e** in **nous mangeons**, remember **le garage**, which starts with a hard **ga** and ends with a soft **ge**. |

3. Verbs ending in **-eler** or **-eter** change as follows:
   (a) Single **l** or single **t** doubles in front of a syllable containing mute **e** because the stress is on that syllable. Examples: **appeler/j'appelle; jeter/je jette**
   (b) Mute **e** changes to **è** when in front of a syllable that contains mute **e** because the stress is on that syllable. Examples: **acheter/j'achète; geler/je gèle**

| Tip | Be careful when pronouncing cognates. For example, in French the **s** in **Israël** is pronounced as an **s**, not a **z** as in the English word Israel. When in doubt, consult an unabridged dictionary. |

§2.

Capitalization, Punctuation Marks, and Word Division

§2.1 CAPITALIZATION

Generally speaking, French capitalization is similar to English in that you must capitalize the first letter of a sentence as well as the names of people and places.

Lundi prochain, Marie va faire un voyage en Afrique. Next Monday, Mary is going to take a trip to Africa.

When they are found elsewhere in a sentence, you must not capitalize days of the week, months of the year (see also §13.3), languages, adjectives of nationality, and religions.

dimanche, lundi, mardi, etc.; janvier, février, mars, etc.; français, espagnol, anglais, etc.; Antonio est italien, María est espagnole; Pierre est français; Jacques est catholique.

However, nouns of nationality are capitalized.
un Américain / an American (male);
une Française / a French woman.

§2.2 PUNCTUATION MARKS

The basic punctuation marks in French are:

le point / period .
le point virgule / semicolon ;
la virgule / comma ,
l'apostrophe (f) / apostrophe '
les deux points / colon :
les parenthèses (f) / parentheses ( )
les guillemets (m) / quotation marks " "
le point d'interrogation / question mark ?
les points de suspension / ellipses points . . .

5

§2.3 WORD DIVISION

It is good to know how to divide a word into syllables (not only in French but also in English) because it helps you pronounce and spell the word correctly.

Basic Rules

- A syllable must contain a vowel, but it may contain only one vowel and no consonant.
  é / cole (*école* / school)

- When you are dealing with single separate consonants, each consonant remains with the vowel that follows it.
  beau / coup (*beaucoup* / many, much)

- When two consonants come together, they are separated; the first remains with the preceding syllable and the second remains with the following syllable.
  im / por / tant (*important*)

But if the second of the two consonants that come together is l or r, do not separate them:
  a / près (*après* / after); *im / meu / ble* (*immeuble* / building, apartment building)

- When three consonants come together, the first two remain with the preceding vowel and the third remains with the vowel that follows it.
  ins / ti / tut (*institut*)

But if the third of the three consonants is l or r, do not separate that third consonant from the second; it remains with the second consonant.
  com / pren / dre (*comprendre* / to understand)

Vowels

• Two vowels together are generally separated if they are strong vowels *(a, e, o)*.

> *a / é / ro / port* (aéroport / airport)

But if you are dealing with a weak vowel *(i, u)*, it ordinarily remains in the same syllable with its neighboring vowel, especially if that other vowel is a strong vowel.

> *huî / tre* (*huître* / oyster)

§2

The Parts of Speech

§3.

Articles, Beginner Level

§3.1 DEFINITE ARTICLE

The definite article in French has four forms, and they all mean "the":

Gender	Singular	Plural
Masculine	*le, l'*	*les*
Feminine	*la, l'*	*les*

Singular	Plural
le garçon / the boy	*les garçons* / the boys
l'arbre (m) / the tree	*les arbres* / the trees
la jeune fille / the girl	*les jeunes filles* / the girls
l'école (f) / the school	*les écoles* / the schools

Definite Article Used

WITH NOUNS

- Before each noun even when more than one noun is stated.
    J'ai le livre et le cahier. / I have the book and notebook.

- When you make a general statement.
    J'aime le lait. / I like milk.

    J'aime l'été. / I like summer.

- With a noun of weight or measure to express "a," "an," "per."
    dix euros le kilo / ten euros per kilo

    vingt euros la douzaine / twenty euros a dozen

- Before a noun indicating a profession, rank, or title followed by the name of the person.
    Le professeur Poulin est absent aujourd'hui. / Professor Poulin is absent today.

- With the name of a language.
    J'étudie le français. / I'm studying French.

EXCEPTION: Do not use the definite article when the name of a language directly follows a form of the verb parler.
    Je parle français et russe. / I speak French and Russian.

However, when the name of the language does not directly follow a form of the verb parler, use the definite article.
    Vous parlez bien l'italien. / You speak Italian well.

- With the days of the week to indicate an action that is habitually repeated.
    Le samedi je vais au cinéma. / On Saturdays I go to the movies.

But when you want to indicate a particular day, do not use the definite article.
    Samedi je vais au cinéma. / Saturday I am going to the movies.
        (understood: <u>this</u> Saturday)

With parts of the body or articles of clothing if the possessor is clearly stated.

> *Luigi, qui est italien, a les cheveux noirs.* / Luigi, who is Italian, has black hair.

With family names in the plural, in which case the spelling of the family name does not change.

> *Nous allons chez les Durand.* / We're going to the Durands.

• When talking about one's body parts, it is common in French to use the definite article instead of a possessive adjective (as we do in English).

> *Mireille s'est cassé le bras en jouant au hockey sur gazon.* / Mireille broke her arm while playing field hockey (see §5.4–5).

§3

WITH PREPOSITIONS

When the prepositions *à* and *de* come before the definite article, it contracts as follows:

Preposition		Article		Contraction
à	+	le	>	au
	+	les	>	aux
de	+	le	>	du
	+	les	>	des

But there is no change with *l'* or *la*.

> *Je vais à l'aéroport.* / I'm going to the airport.
> *Je vais à la bibliothèque.* / I'm going to the library.
> *Je viens de l'aéroport.* / I'm coming from the airport.
> *Je viens de la bibliothèque.* / I'm coming from the library.

With the preposition *à* (which combines to form *au* or *aux*) in front of the name of a country that is masculine.

>   *Nous allons au Canada.* / We're going to Canada.
>
>   *Janine vient aux États-Unis.* / Janine is coming to the United States.

With the preposition *de* (which combines to form *du* or *des*) before the name of a country that is masculine.

>   *du Portugal* / from Portugal
>
>   *des Etats-Unis* / from the United States

 Tip For some countries that do not normally use a definite article, for example, *Haïti* and *Israël*, you do not need to make this contraction.

>   *Maximilien vient d'Haïti.* / Maximilian is from Haiti.

With the preposition *de* + a common noun to indicate possession.

>   *le livre du garçon* / the boy's book
>
>   *les livres des garçons* / the boys' books
>
>   *la robe de la jeune fille* / the girl's dress
>
>   *les poupées des petites filles* / the little girls' dolls

WITH CERTAIN EXPRESSIONS

- Indicating segments of the day.

>   *l'après-midi* / in the afternoon; *le matin* / in the morning; *le soir* / in the evening

- Common expressions.

>   *à l'école* / to school, in school; *à la maison* / at home
>
>   *la semaine dernière* / last week; *l'année dernière* / last year
>
>   *la plupart de* / most of
>
>   *la plupart des jeunes filles* / most of the girls

- As a partitive in the affirmative.

>   *J'ai du café.* / I have (some) coffee.
>
>   *Tu as de l'argent.* / You have (some) money.
>
>   *Il a des amis.* / He has friends.

Definite Article Not Used

However, the definite article is *not* used when the partitive is in the negative or when the definite article is used with an adjective.

Je n'ai pas de café. / I haven't any coffee.

Tu n'as pas d'argent. / You haven't any money.

Il a de bons amis. / He has some good friends.

Do not use the definite article:

§3

In direct address: *Bonjour, docteur Leduc.*

After the preposition *en*: *Nous écrivons en français.*
Exceptions:

en l'air / in the air; *en l'absence de* / in the absence of; *en l'honneur de* / in honor of

After the preposition *de* in an adjective phrase: *J'aime mon livre de français.*

With a feminine country and continents when you use *en* / at, to or *de* / of, from.

Je vais en France, en Angleterre, en Allemagne, en Australie, en Asie, et en Amérique.

Paul vient de France, les Armstrong viennent d'Australie et Hilda vient d'Allemagne.

With most cities: *à Paris, à New York; de Londres, de Montréal, de Sydney.*

However, when a city name begins with a masculine definite article (for example, *Le Mans* and *Le Havre*), you must make the usual contraction with the prepositions *à* and *de.*

Les 24 heures du Mans auront lieu en juin au Mans. / The 24 Hours of Le Mans will take place in June in Le Mans.

With a noun in apposition: *Paul, fils du professeur Leblanc, est très aimable.*

With titles of monarchs:

Louis Seize (Louis XVI). / Louis the Sixteenth.

With the preposition *sans* or with the construction *ne . . . ni . . . ni . . . :*

> *Je n'ai ni papier ni stylo.* / I have neither paper nor pen.
> *Il est parti sans argent.* / He left without money.

With certain expressions of quantity that take *de*: *beaucoup de, trop de, combien de, peu de, plus de, assez de*

> *Marie a beaucoup d'amis.* / Marie has a lot of (many) friends.

With the preposition *avec* when the noun after it is abstract:

> *Jean-Luc parle avec enthousiasme.*
> *Tu viens avec nous?* / Are you coming with us?
> *Avec plaisir!* / With pleasure!

§3.2 INDEFINITE ARTICLE

The forms of the indefinite article are:

Singular

J'ai un frère. / I have a brother.
J'ai une sœur. / I have a sister.

Plural

J'ai des frères. / I have brothers.
J'ai des sœurs. / I have sisters.

The indefinite article is used:

- When you want to say "a" or "an." It is also used as a numeral to mean "one":
  un livre / a book or one book
  une orange / an orange or one orange

- In front of each noun in a series:
  J'ai un cahier, un crayon et une gomme. / I have a notebook, pencil, and eraser.

• With *C'est* or *Ce sont* with or without an adjective:

    C'est un docteur. / He's a doctor.

    C'est un mauvais docteur. / He's a bad doctor.

    Ce sont des étudiants. / They are students.

However, if you are being specific, you still use the definite article:

    C'est l'avocate qui m'a aidé à préparer mon testament. / She is the attorney who helped me to prepare my will.

The indefinite article is *not* used:

• With *cent* and *mille*:

    J'ai cent dollars. / I have a hundred dollars.

    J'ai mille dollars. / I have a thousand dollars.

• With *il est, ils sont, elle est, elles sont* + an unmodified noun of nationality, profession, or religion:

    Elle est professeur. / She is a professor.

    Il est catholique. / He is (a) Catholic.

When you use *quel* in an exclamation:

    Quelle femme! / What a woman!

    Quel homme! / What a man!

With negations, particularly with the verb *avoir*:

    Avez-vous un livre? Non, je n'ai pas de livre. / Have you a book? No, I don't have a book (any book).

§3.3 PARTITIVE

The partitive denotes a *part* of a whole; in other words, some. In English, we express the partitive by saying "some" or "any" in front of the noun. Use the following forms in front of the noun:

    Masculine singular: *du* or *de l'*

    Feminine singular: *de la* or *de l'*

    Masculine or feminine plural: *des*

Tip

If the thing you are talking about can be counted individually, you should not use the partitive.
You should use the indefinite article: **J'ai des bonbons.** / I have some candy. (You can eat a single **bonbon**.)

Simple Affirmative

J'ai **du** *café.* / I have some coffee.
J'ai **de la** *viande.* / I have some meat.
J'ai **de l'***eau.* / I have some water.

There can be a partitive in the plural as long as you are not, in fact, talking about something countable.

Je mange **des** *pâtes.* / I am eating pasta.

Simple Negative

Je **n'***ai* **pas de** *café.* / I don't have any coffee.
Je **n'***ai* **pas de** *viande.* / I don't have any meat.
Je **n'***ai* **pas d'***eau.* / I don't have any water.
Je **n'***ai* **pas d'***épinards.* / I don't have any spinach.
Je **n'***ai* **pas de** *pâtes.* / I don't have any pasta.

Tip

If you have trouble remembering this rule, when someone says, *"Merci!"* get in the habit of saying, *"Il n'y a pas de quoi!"* or *"Pas de quoi"* so that *"pas de"* becomes second nature for you.

Tip

For the verb *être* in the negative, you do not need to make this change. *Ce n'est pas une mauvaise idée.* / That isn't a bad idea.

With an Adjective

> *J'ai de jolis chapeaux.* / I have some pretty hats.
> *J'ai de jolies robes.* / I have some pretty dresses.

Note the following:

- When the noun is preceded by an adverb or noun of quantity or measure, use *de*, as in *J'ai beaucoup de choses.* / I have many things.
- When the noun is modified by another noun, use *de*, as in *une école de danse* / a school of dance.
- The partitive is not used with *sans* or *ne . . . ni . . . ni.*

  Example:
  J'ai quitté la maison sans argent. / I left the house without any money.

- Use *quelques* and not the partitive when by "some" you mean "a few," in other words, "not many."

  Examples:
  J'ai quelques amis. / I have a few (some) friends.
  J'ai quelques bonbons. / I have a few (some) candies.

- When the negated verb is *ne . . . que* / only, the partitive consists of *de* plus the definite article.

  Examples:
  Elle ne lit que des livres électroniques. / She reads only e-books.

  Laure est végétarienne. Elle ne mange que des légumes. / Laura is a vegetarian. She eats only vegetables.

- The partitive must be repeated before each noun.

  Example:
  Ici on vend du papier, de l'encre et des cahiers. / Here they sell paper, ink, and notebooks.

§3

Tip

When you are ordering food, it is possible to use an indefinite article to refer to the serving.
Un café, s'il vous plaît. / A (cup of) coffee, please.

 Tip

You can also use the definite article when ordering a specific item listed on a menu.
Le poulet à l'orange, s'il vous plaît. / The orange chicken, please.

§4.

Nouns, Beginner Level

§4.1 GENDER

A *noun* is a word that refers to a person, place, thing, or quality. Nouns are either masculine or feminine and require the article *le, la, l'*, or *les*. The gender of many nouns that refer to persons or animals is obvious. However, nouns that refer to some animals are not always evident. (See below.)

Examples

PERSONS	
Masculine	**Feminine**
l'homme / the man	la femme / the woman
le garçon / the boy	*la jeune fille* / the girl
l'oncle / the uncle	*la tante* / the aunt

ANIMALS	
Masculine	**Feminine**
le taureau / the bull	*la vache* / the cow
le coq / the rooster	*la poule* / the hen
le chat / the cat	*la chatte* / the cat
le chien / the dog	*la chienne* / the dog
le loup / the wolf	*la louve* / the wolf, she-wolf

Sometimes the gender of a noun does not match the gender of the animal to which it refers. Here are a few examples:

une chèvre / a goat
un crocodile / a crocodile
une girafe / a giraffe
une sauterelle / a grasshopper
une souris / a mouse

• The gender of nouns referring to anything other than persons or animals must be learned with the noun.

Examples

Gender	Noun Endings	Examples
Masculine	-age or -âge	*l'âge* / age
		le fromage / cheese
	-ment	*le logement* / lodging
		le médicament / medicine (you take)
	-eau	*le chapeau* / hat
		le gâteau / cake
Feminine	-ance	*la circonstance* / circumstance
		la chance / chance, luck
	-ence	*l'apparence* / appearance
		la science / science
	-tion	*l'attention* / attention
		la notion / idea, notion
	-ette	*la fourchette* / fork
		la serviette / napkin
		la sucette / lollipop

Tip	Although the *-eau* ending is masculine, *l'eau* / water is feminine. Similarly, although the *-ette* ending is typically feminine, *le squelette* / skeleton is masculine.

Special Cases

Some nouns have one meaning when masculine, another meaning when feminine:

Masculine	**Feminine**
le critique / critic	*la critique* / criticism
le livre / book	*la livre* / pound
le manche / handle	*la manche* / sleeve
le poêle / wood stove	*la poêle* / frying pan
le poste / job	*la poste* / mail, post office
le somme / nap	*la somme* / sum total
le tour / turn, tour	*la tour* / tower
le vase / vase	*la vase* / mud
le voile / veil	*la voile* / sail

§4

Tip	It helps to associate a difficult noun with an image or with an adjective that changes according to gender. For example, to remember if you need to say *le manche* or *la manche*, you may picture a person in a short-sleeved shirt *(une chemise à manches courtes)* standing by the English Channel *(La Manche)*. The important thing is for the image to have meaning for you.

Some nouns are the same for both:

Masculine	**Feminine**
un élève / pupil (boy)	*une élève* / pupil (girl)
un enfant / child (boy)	*une enfant* / child (girl)

Some nouns add *-e* to the masculine to form the feminine:

Masculine	**Feminine**
un cousin / cousin	*une cousine* / cousin
un ami / friend	*une amie* / friend

Some nouns change the *-eur* masculine ending to *-euse* for feminine:

Masculine	**Feminine**
un vendeur / salesman	*une vendeuse* / saleswoman
un menteur / liar	*une menteuse* / liar
le serveur / server	*la serveuse* / server

Some masculine *-teur* nouns change to *-trice* in the feminine:

un acteur / actor	*une actrice*
un aviateur / aviator	*une aviatrice*
un spectateur / spectator	*une spectatrice*

In your studies, if you are not sure of the feminine form of a French noun or adjective in the singular or plural, you must get into the habit of looking up words in a dictionary.

§4.2 PLURAL OF NOUNS—THE BASICS

Add *-s* to the singular:

Singular	**Plural**
le livre / the book	*les livres* / the books
la maison / the house	*les maisons* / the houses
l'étudiant / the student	*les étudiants* / the students

If a noun ends in *-s, -x,* or *-z* in the singular, leave it alone:

Singular	**Plural**
le bras / the arm	*les livres* / the books
la voix / the voice	*les voix* / the voices
le nez / the nose	*les nez* / the noses

If a noun ends in *-al* in the singular, change *-al* to *-aux:*

Singular

le journal / the newspaper
le canal / the canal

Plural

les journaux / the newspapers
les canaux / the canals
Exception:
le festival / the festival   *les festivals* / the festivals

---

§4

If a noun ends in *-eu* or *-eau* in the singular, add *-x:*

Singular

le feu / the fire
le bureau / the office, the desk
le jeu / the game

Plural

les feux / the fires
les bureaux / the offices, the desks
les jeux / the games
Exception:
le pneu / the tire   *les pneus* / the tires

Common irregular nouns

Singular	**Plural**
le ciel / the sky	*les cieux* / the skies
l'œil / the eye	*les yeux* / the eyes

§5.

Adjectives, Beginner Level

§5.1 FORMATION

Feminine Singular

The feminine singular of an adjective is normally formed by adding *-e* to the masculine singular.

Examples:

joli—jolie / pretty   *présent—présente* / present

grand—grande / tall

If a masculine singular adjective already ends in *-e*, the feminine singular is the same form.

Examples:

aimable / kind   *énorme* / huge   *faible* / weak

Some feminine singular forms are irregular. If a masculine singular adjective ends in *-c*, change it to *-que* for the feminine; *-er* to *-ère*; *-f* to *-ve*; *-g* to *-gue*; and *-x* to *-se*.

Examples:

public—publique / public   *long—longue* / long

premier—première / first   *heureux—heureuse* / happy

actif—active / active

Some masculine singular adjectives double the final consonant before adding *-e* to form the feminine.

Examples:

ancien—ancienne / old   *cruel—cruelle* / cruel
bas—basse / low   *gentil—gentille* / kind, nice
bon—bonne / good   *sot—sotte* / foolish
pareil—pareille / similar   *épais—épaisse* / thick

25

• The following feminine singular adjectives are formed from the irregular masculine singular forms:

Masculine Singular Before a Masculine Singular Noun Beginning with a Consonant	Irregular Masculine Singular Before a Masculine Singular Noun Beginning with a Vowel or Silent H
beau / beautiful, handsome	*un bel ami*
fou / crazy	*un fol ami*
nouveau / new	*un nouvel hôtel*
vieux / old	*un vieil ami*

Feminine Singular
une belle amie
une folle amie
une nouvelle amie
une vieille amie

> **Tip** *La vieille dame a passé la veille de Noël avec son vieil ami dans un vieux cabaret.* / The old lady spent Christmas Eve with her old friend in an old cabaret.

• Some common masculine singular adjectives have irregular forms in the feminine singular. These do not fall into any particular category like those above.

Examples:

blanc—blanche / white
complet—complète / complete
doux—douce / soft, smooth, sweet
faux—fausse / false
favori—favorite / favorite
frais—fraîche / fresh
sec—sèche / dry

Plural

- The plural is normally formed by adding *-s* to the masculine or feminine singular.

   Examples:
   bon—bons; bonne—bonnes / good   *joli—jolis; jolie—jolies* / pretty

- If the masculine singular already ends in *-s* or *-x*, it remains the same in the masculine plural.

   Examples:
   gris—gris / gray   *heureux—heureux* / happy
   Mon oncle a les cheveux gris. / My uncle has gray hair.

- If a masculine singular adjective ends in *-al*, it changes to *-aux* (with some exceptions).

   Examples:
   égal—égaux / equal   *principal—principaux* / principal
   Exceptions: *fatal—fatals* / fatal   *natal—natals* / native

- If a masculine singular adjective ends in *-eau*, it changes to *-eaux*.

   Examples:
   nouveau—nouveaux / new   *beau—beaux* / beautiful, handsome

§5.2 AGREEMENT

An adjective agrees in gender (feminine or masculine) and number (singular or plural) with the noun or pronoun it modifies. If the verb is a form of *être* (to be), an agreement is made on the adjective with the subject.

   Examples:
   Alexandre et Théodore sont beaux et intelligents. / Alexander and
      Theodore are handsome and smart.
   Yolande est belle. / Yolande is beautiful.
   Janine et Monique sont belles. / Janine and Monique are beautiful.
   Hélène et Simone sont actives. / Helene and Simone are active.
   Anne est jolie. / Anne is pretty.
   C'est un bel arbre. / It is a beautiful tree.

§5

Ils sont amusants. / They are amusing.

Chaque garçon est présent. / Every boy is here (present).

Chaque jeune fille est présente. / Every girl is here (present).

Valentine est absente. / Valentine is absent.

Note that you must use the masculine plural form of the adjective when it modifies nouns, proper nouns, or pronouns of mixed gender: *Daniel et Danielle sont américains.* / Daniel and Danielle are American.

§5.3 POSITION

- In French, most descriptive adjectives are placed after the noun; e.g., colors, nationality, religion: *une robe blanche* / a white dress, *un fromage français* / a French cheese, *une femme catholique* / a Catholic woman

- Here are some examples of common short adjectives that are generally placed in front of the noun:
  un autre livre / another book, *un bel arbre* / a beautiful tree, *un beau cadeau* / a beautiful gift, *un bon dîner* / a good dinner, *chaque jour* / each day, *un gros livre* / a big book, *une jeune dame* / a young lady, *une jolie maison* / a pretty house, *une petite table* / a small table, *plusieurs amis* / several friends, *un vieil homme* / an old man, *le premier rang* / the first row, *quelques bonbons* / some candy, *un tel garçon* / such a boy.

- Some adjectives change in meaning, depending on whether the adjective is in front of the noun or after it. The most common are:

la semaine dernière / last week	*la dernière semaine* / the last (final) week
ma robe propre / my clean dress	*ma propre robe* / my own dress
une femme brave / a brave woman	*une brave femme* / a fine woman
le moment même / the very moment	*le même moment* / the same moment
un livre cher / an expensive book	*un cher ami* / a dear friend
un homme grand / a tall man	*un grand homme* / a great man

§5.4 TYPES

§5.4–1 Descriptive

A descriptive adjective is a word that describes a noun or pronoun: *une belle maison* / a beautiful house, *un beau livre* / a beautiful book, *un bel arbre* / a beautiful tree, *une jolie femme* / a pretty woman, *un chapeau gris* / a gray hat, *une jupe bleue* / a blue skirt, *une femme brave* / a brave woman.

Elle est grande. / She is tall.

§5.4–2 Demonstrative

A demonstrative adjective is used to point out something or someone.

Gender	Singular	Plural
Masculine	*ce, cet* / this, that	*ces* / these, those
Feminine	*cette* / this, that	*ces* / these, those

Examples:
Ce garçon est beau. / This boy is handsome.
Cet arbre est beau. / This tree is beautiful.
Cette femme est belle. / This woman is beautiful.
Ces hommes sont beaux. / These men are handsome.
Ces livres sont beaux. / These books are beautiful.
Ces dames sont belles. / These ladies are beautiful.

Tip If you wish to make a contrast between "this" and "that" or "these" and "those," add *-ci* this, these or *-là* that, those to the noun with a hyphen.

Ce garçon-ci est plus fort que ce garçon-là. / This boy is stronger than that boy.

The form *cet* is used in front of a masculine singular noun or adjective beginning with a vowel or silent *h: cet arbre, cet homme.*

§5

If there is more than one noun, a demonstrative adjective must be used in front of each noun: *cette dame et ce monsieur.*

§5.4–3 Interrogative

The adjective *quel* is generally regarded as interrogative because it is frequently used in a question. Its forms are *quel, quelle, quels, quelles.* Note that in English the translation is *which* or *what.*

Examples:

Quel livre voulez-vous? / Which book do you want?
Quel est votre nom? / What is your name?
Quelle heure est-il? / What time is it?
Quelle est votre adresse? / What is your address?
Quels sont les mois de l'année? / What are the months of the year?
Quelles sont les saisons? / What are the seasons?

The adjective *quel* is also used in exclamations. Note that the indefinite article *un (une)* is not used in this case.

Examples:

Quel garçon! / What a boy!
Quelle jeune fille! / What a girl!
Quel bruit! / What a noise!

§5.4–4 Possessive

MASCULINE	
Singular	**Plural**
mon livre / my book	*mes livres* / my books
ton stylo / your pen	*tes stylos* / your pens
son ballon / his (her, its) balloon	*ses ballons* / his (her, its) balloons
notre parapluie / our umbrella	*nos parapluies* / our umbrellas
votre sandwich / your sandwich	*vos sandwichs* / your sandwiches
leur gâteau / their cake	*leurs gâteaux* / their cakes

FEMININE	
Singular	**Plural**
ma robe / my dress	*mes robes* / my dresses
ta veste / your jacket	*tes vestes* / your jackets
sa balle / his (her, its) ball	*ses balles* / his (her, its) balls
notre maison / our house	*nos maisons* / our houses
votre voiture / your car	*vos voitures* / your cars
leur sœur / their sister	*leurs sœurs* / their sisters

- A possessive adjective agrees in gender and number with the noun it modifies.
- *Notre*, *votre*, and *leur* do not agree with the gender of the noun in the singular. They are all the same, whether in front of a masculine or feminine singular noun.
- Possessive adjectives do not agree with the gender of the noun in the plural. They are all the same, whether in front of a masculine or feminine plural noun: *mes, tes, ses, nos, vos, leurs*.
- Be aware of *mon (ma), ton (ta), son (sa)*: In front of a feminine singular noun beginning with a vowel or silent *h*, the masculine singular forms are used: *mon, ton, son* —not *ma, ta, sa*.

mon adresse / my address
ton opinion / your opinion
son amie / his (or her) friend
mon habitude / my habit (custom)

 Tip   Since *son, sa*, and *ses* can mean "his" or "her," you may add *à lui* or *à elle* to make the meaning clear.

§5

> *sa maison à lui* / his house
> *sa maison à elle* / her house
> *son livre à lui* / his book
> *son livre à elle* / her book
> *ses livres à lui* / his books
> *ses livres à elle* / her books

| Tip | If there is more than one noun, a possessive adjective must be used in front of each noun: *ma mère et mon père, mon livre et mon cahier.* |

§5.4–5 Possessive Adjectives with Parts of the Body and Clothing

* When using the verb *avoir*, the definite article is normally used with parts of the body, *not* the possessive adjective.
   Henri a les mains sales. / Henry has dirty hands.
   Simone a les cheveux roux. / Simone has red hair.

* When using a reflexive verb, the definite article is normally used, **not** the possessive adjective.
   Paulette s'est lavé les cheveux. / Paulette washed her hair.

Note that there is no feminine agreement on *lavé*. This is because the direct object is *les cheveux*. What did she wash? She washed her hair. In the statement, "*Paulette s'est lavée*," an *e* is added to *lavé* because the action reflects back on Paulette; the *s'* (*se*) is therefore a preceding direct object pronoun. What did she wash? She washed herself.

   See §22, Agreement of Past Participle of a Reflexive Verb with its Reflexive Pronoun (see also §3).

* The *definite article* is used instead of the possessive adjective when referring to parts of the body or clothing if it is clear who the possessor is.
   Henri tient le livre dans la main. / Henry is holding the book in his hand.

§5.4–6 Comparative and Superlative

Comparative

Of the same degree: *aussi . . . que* / as . . . as
Of a lesser degree: *moins . . . que* / less . . . than
Of a higher degree: *plus . . . que* / more . . . than

>*Janine est aussi grande que Monique.* / Janine is as tall as Monique.
>*Monique est moins travailleuse que Janine.* / Monique is less
>   hard-working than Janine.
>*Janine est plus sportive que Monique.* / Janine is more athletic than
>   Monique.

• *Aussi . . . que* often becomes *si . . . que* in a negative sentence.
>*Robert n'est pas si grand que Joseph.* / Robert is not as tall
>   as Joseph.

>This change is not always made. You may also hear or read:
>   Robert n'est pas **aussi** grand que Joseph.

The comparative and superlative forms of the adjective "bad"
are irregular. To say "worse" you can say *pire* or *plus
mauvais(e).* "The worst" is *le/la pire* or *le/la plus mauvais(e).*
It is more proper to say *pire* or *le/la pire,* but *plus mauvais,
plus mauvaise, le plus mauvais,* and *la plus mauvaise,* are also
used by native speakers.

>*Ce portable est mauvais.* / This cell phone is bad.
>*Ce portable est plus mauvais que l'autre.* OR *Ce portable est pire
>   que l'autre.* / This cell phone is worse than the other.

>*Ce portable est le plus mauvais.* OR *Ce portable est le pire.* / This
>   cell phone is the worst.

>The plural form is *pires* OR *les pires* / *les plus mauvais(es).*
>*Ces chaussures sont plus mauvaises que les autres.* OR *Ces chaus-
>   sures sont pires que les autres.* / These shoes are worse than
>   the others.

>*Ces portables sont les plus mauvais.* OR *Ces portables sont les
>   pires.* / These cell phones are the worst.

>*Ces chaussures sont les plus mauvaises.* OR *Ces chaussures sont
>   les pires.* / These shoes are the worst.

§5

• *Plus que* / more than becomes *plus de* + a number.

   Examples:
   > *Il a plus de cinquante ans.* / He is more than fifty years old.
   > *Je lui ai donné plus de cent dollars.* / I gave him (her) more than a
   > hundred dollars.

Superlative

• The superlative is formed by placing the appropriate definite
  article *(le, la, les)* in front of the comparative:
   > *Marie est la plus grande jeune fille de la classe.* / Mary is the
   > tallest girl in the class.

• If the adjective normally follows the noun, the definite article
  must be used twice—in front of the noun and in front of the
  superlative:
   > *Monsieur Hibou fut le président le plus sage de la nation.* /
   > Mr. Hibou was the wisest president of the nation.

• After a superlative, the preposition *de* (not *dans*) is normally
  used to express "in":
   > *Pierre est le plus jeune garçon de la classe.* / Peter is the youngest
   > boy in the class.

• If more than one comparative or superlative is expressed,
  each is repeated:
   > *Marie est la plus intelligente et la plus sérieuse de l'école.* / Mary is
   > the most intelligent and most serious in the school.

Tip	*Une devinette* (a riddle) using a superlative:

Quelle est la chose la plus sale de la maison? / What
is the dirtiest thing in the house?
un balai / a broom

Irregular Comparative and Superlative Adjectives

Adjective (m)	Comparative	Superlative
bon / good	*meilleur* / better	*le meilleur* / (the) best
mauvais / bad	*plus mauvais* } *pire* } worse	*le plus mauvais* } *le pire* } (the) worst
petit / small	*plus petit* / smaller (in size) *moindre* / less (in importance)	*le plus petit* / (the) smallest *le moindre* / (the) least

§5.4–7 Meilleur and Mieux

Meilleur is an adjective and must agree in gender and number with the noun or pronoun it modifies.

Example:
Cette pomme est bonne, cette pomme-là est meilleure que celle-ci et celle-là est la meilleure. / This apple is good, that apple is better than this one, and that one is the best.

Mieux is an adverb and does not change in form for gender or number.

Example:
Marie chante bien, Anne chante mieux que Marie et Claire chante le mieux. / Mary sings well, Anne sings better than Mary, and Claire sings the best.

 The adverb *bien* / well and the adverb *mieux* / better both contain *ie*.

Mieux is also an adjective and does not change in form.

Examples:
C'est mieux que jamais. / It's better than ever.

Pierre est mieux avec les cheveux longs. / Pierre looks better with long hair.

§5.4–8 Adjectives Used in an Adverbial Sense

An adjective used as an adverb does not normally change in form.
Cette rose sent bon. / This rose smells good.
Ces bonbons coûtent cher. / These candies are expensive.

§6.

Pronouns, Beginner, Intermediate, and Advanced Levels

§6.1 TYPES

§6.1–1 Subject Pronouns

The subject pronouns are:

Person	Singular	Plural
1st	*je (j')* / I	*nous* / we
2nd	*tu* / you (familiar)	*vous* / you (singular polite or plural)
3rd	*il* / he, it *elle* / she, it *on* / one	*ils* / they *(m.)* *elles* / they *(f.)*

- Note that *je* becomes *j'* before a vowel or a silent *h:*
  j'aime / I love; *j'hésite* / I hesitate.
- Note that the masculine plural pronoun *ils* is used when there is at least one masculine noun or male individual in a pair or group. The adjective is also masculine plural:
  Richard et Lucille sont canadiens. → *Ils* sont canadiens. / They are Canadian.

Tip

Remember that *vous* is not always plural; it is also the polite form of the second person; *tu* is the familiar form. You can use the *tu* form with members of the family and close friends, but always use the *vous* form with strangers and with people you do not know well.You should also use the *tu* form with pets, even if you don't know them well!

§6.1–2 Direct Object Pronouns

The direct object pronouns are:

Person	Singular
1st	*me (m')* / me
2nd	*te (t')* / you (familiar)
3rd	$\begin{cases} \textit{le (l')} \text{ / him, it} \\ \textit{la (l')} \text{ / her, it} \end{cases}$ (person or thing)

Person	Plural
1st	*nous* / us
2nd	*vous* / you (singular polite or plural)
3rd	*les* / them (persons or things)

- A direct object pronoun takes the place of a direct object noun.
- A direct object noun ordinarily comes after the verb, but a direct object pronoun is ordinarily placed *in front* of the verb or infinitive. For the position of direct and indirect object pronouns in different types of sentences, see §11.2 to §11.5.

Examples:

J'ai les lettres. / I have the letters. → *Je les ai.* / I have them.
Je connais Luigi. / I know Luigi. → *Je le connais.* / I know him.

> | Tip | *Je lis la leçon.* / I'm reading the lesson. Drop the noun *leçon;* what remains is *la*, the feminine singular definite article. It now becomes the direct object pronoun. Place it in front of the verb; *Je la lis.* / I'm reading it. |

• *Me, te, le,* and *la* become *m', t', l'* when directly followed by a verb that starts with a vowel or silent *h*.

Elle a le portable. / She has the cell phone.
Elle l'a. / She has it.
Est-ce que tu m'aimes? / Do you love me?
Oui, je t'aime beaucoup. / Yes, I love you a lot.

§6.1–3 Indirect Object Pronouns

The indirect object pronouns are:

Person	Singular	
1st	*me (m')*	to me
2nd	*te (t')*	to you (familiar)
3rd	*lui*	to him, to her

Person	Plural	
1st	*nous*	to us
2nd	*vous*	to you (singular polite or plural)
3rd	*leur*	to them

§6

- An indirect object pronoun takes the place of an indirect object noun. An indirect object noun is a noun that is used as an indirect object. Example: I am talking to Mary. In that sentence Mary is an indirect object noun because it is preceded by the preposition "to"; as an indirect object pronoun, one would say "to her" in place of "to Mary."
- An indirect object pronoun is ordinarily placed *in front* of the verb. For the position of direct and indirect object pronouns in different types of sentences, see §11.2 to §11.5.

  Examples:
  Je parle à Janine. / I'm talking to Janine. → *Je lui parle.* / I'm talking to her.
  Je parle à Luigi et à mon ami. / I'm talking to Luigi and my friend. → *Je leur parle.* / I'm talking to them.

Note that the preposition *à* is repeated in the second sentence: *à Luigi et à mon ami.*

§6.1–4 Double Object Pronouns

Tip

To get a picture of what the word order is when you have more than one object pronoun (direct and indirect) in a sentence, see Order of Elements in French Sentences, §11.2 to §11.5.

§6.1–5 *En*

- The pronoun *en* takes the place of the partitive and serves as a direct object. It can refer to persons or things.

  Examples:
  Avez-vous des frères? / Do you have any brothers?
  Oui, j'en ai. / Yes, I have (some).
  Avez-vous de l'argent? / Have you any money?
  Oui, j'en ai. / Yes, I have (some). *Non, je n'en ai pas.* / No, I don't have any.

- The past participle of a compound verb does not agree with the preceding direct object *en.* See also the last paragraph in §7.1.

  Avez-vous écrit des lettres? / Did you write any letters? *Oui, j'en ai écrit trois.* / Yes, I wrote three (of them).

- When using a reflexive verb, use *en* to take the place of the preposition *de* + a thing.

  Est-ce que vous vous souvenez de l'adresse? / Do you remember the address?

  Oui, je m'en souviens. / Yes, I remember it.

  Est-ce que vous vous servez des hors-d'œuvre? / Are you helping yourself to the hors d'œuvre?

  Oui, merci, je m'en sers. / Yes, thank you, I'm helping myself to some.

  Do not use *en* to take the place of the preposition *de* + a person. Use a disjunctive pronoun (see §6.1–7).

  Est-ce que vous vous souvenez de cette dame? / Do you remember this lady?

  Oui, je me souviens d'elle. / Yes, I remember her.

- Use *en* to take the place of *de* + noun and retain the word of quantity.

  Avez-vous beaucoup d'amis? / Do you have many friends?

  Oui, j'en ai beaucoup. / Yes, I have many (of them).

  Madame Paquet a-t-elle mis trop de sel dans le ragoût? / Did Mrs. Paquet put too much salt in the stew?

  Oui, elle en a mis trop dans le ragoût. / Yes, she put too much (of it) in the stew.

- Use *en* to take the place of the preposition *de* + the place to mean "from there."

  Est-ce que vous venez de l'école? / Are you coming from school?

  Oui, j'en viens. / Yes, I'm coming from there.

  Non, je n'en viens pas. / No, I am not coming from there.

§6

§6.1–6 *Y*

Use *y* as a pronoun to serve as an object replacing a prepositional phrase beginning with *à, dans, sur,* or *chez* that refers to things, places, or ideas.

Est-ce que vous pensez à l'examen? / Are you thinking of the exam?

Oui, j'y pense. / Yes, I'm thinking of it.

Je réponds à la lettre. / I'm answering the letter.

J'y réponds. / I'm answering it.

Est-ce que les fleurs sont sur la table? / Are the flowers on the table?

Oui, elles y sont. / Yes, they are there.

Est-ce que vous allez chez Pierre? / Are you going to Pierre's?

Oui, j'y vais. / Yes, I'm going (there).

§6.1–7 Disjunctive Pronouns

Person	Singular	Plural
1st	*moi* me, I	*nous* us, we
2nd	*toi* you (familiar)	*vous* you (formal singular or plural)
3rd	*soi* oneself *lui* him, he *elle* her, she	*eux* them, they (m.) *elles* them, they (f.)

Examples:

Je vais chez moi. / I'm going to my house.

Tu vas chez toi. / You're going to your house.

Il va chez lui. / He's going to his house.

Elle va chez elle. / She's going to her house.

On va chez soi. / One is going to one's own house.

Nous allons chez nous. / We're going to our house.

Vous allez chez vous. / You're going to your house.

Ils vont chez eux. / They're going to their house.

Elles vont chez elles. / They're going to their house.

A disjunctive pronoun is used:

* as object of a preposition.
  Elle parle avec moi. / She is talking with me.
  Je pense toujours à toi. / I always think of you.

* in a compound subject or object.
  Elle et lui sont amoureux. / He and she are in love.
  Je vous connais—toi et lui. / I know you—you and him.

* for emphasis.
  Moi, je parle bien; lui, il ne parle pas bien. / I speak well; he does not speak well.

* to indicate possession with *à* if the verb is *être* and if the subject is a noun, personal pronoun, or demonstrative pronoun.
  Ce livre est à moi. / This book is mine.
  Je suis à toi. / I am yours.

* with *c'est* and *ce sont*.
  Qui est à la porte?—C'est moi. / Who is at the door? It is I.
  C'est toi? Oui, c'est moi. / Is it you? Yes, it is I.
  Est-ce que ce sont eux?—Oui, ce sont eux. / Is it they?—Yes it's they.

Tip

In spoken English we often say, "It's me. It's her. It's him," and so on instead of "It is I. It is she. It is he." In French, one must always say, "*C'est moi. C'est elle. C'est lui,*" and so on.

---

* with *même* and *mêmes*.
  Est-ce Pierre?—Oui, c'est lui-même. / Is it Peter? Yes, it's he himself.

  Vont-ils les manger eux-mêmes? / Are they going to eat them themselves?

Tip

When you answer the telephone and the caller asks for you by name, you may answer with, "*C'est moi-même.*"
Bonjour, Madame Beaupuy, s'il vous plaît. / Hello, Mrs. Beaupuy, please.
C'est moi-même. / That's me. OR Speaking.

• when no verb is stated.

> *Qui est à l'appareil? Moi.* / Who is on the phone? I (am).

> *Qui a brisé le vase? Eux.* / Who broke the vase? They (did).

See also Order of Elements in French Sentences, §11.

§6.1–8 Demonstrative Pronouns

The demonstrative pronouns are:

	Singular	**Plural**
Masculine	*celui* / the one	*ceux* / the ones
Feminine	*celle* / the one	*celles* / the ones

Each demonstrative pronoun must match its corresponding noun in both gender and number.

Examples:

J'ai mangé mon gâteau et celui de Pierre. / I ate my cake and Peter's.

Il aime beaucoup ma voiture et celle de Jacques. / He likes my car very much and Jack's.

J'ai mangé mes petits pois et ceux de David. / I ate my peas and David's.

J'aime tes jupes et celles de Jeanne. / I like your skirts and Joan's.

J'ai deux éclairs; est-ce que tu préfères celui-ci ou celui-là? / I have two eclairs; do you prefer this one or that one?

J'ai deux pommes; est-ce que tu préfères celle-ci ou celle-là? / I have two apples; do you prefer this one or that one?

Tip

Quel chapeau? Celui que tu as acheté. / Which hat? The one (that) you bought.

Note that in English we do not have to say *that*, but in French we must say *que* because a new clause follows.

Tip

Quelles fleurs? Celles que tu m'as données. / Which flowers? The ones (that) you gave me.

Tip	**BUT:**

Qui l'a fait? C'est lui qui l'a fait. / Who did it? He's the one who did it.

Tip	*C'est elle qui l'a dit.* / She's the one who said it.

See §6.1–7.

ce (c'), ceci, cela, ça

These are demonstrative pronouns but they are invariable; that is, they do not change in gender and number. They refer to things that are not identified by name and may refer to an idea or a statement mentioned.

Examples:
C'est vrai. / It's true.
*Ceci est vrai. / This is true. *Ceci est faux.* / This is false.
*Cela est vrai. / That is true. *Cela est faux.* / That is false.
Ça m'intéresse beaucoup. / That interests me very much.
Qu'est-ce que c'est que cela? or *Qu'est-ce que c'est que ça?* / What's that?

Note that *cela* shortens to *ça* when used informally.
* Note also that *ceci* refers to what follows and *cela* to what was stated.

§6.1–9 Indefinite Pronouns

aucun (aucune) / not any, not one, none
un autre (une autre) / another, another one
nous autres Français / we French (people)
nous autres Américains / we American (people)
certains (certaines) / certain ones
chacun (chacune) / each one
nul (nulle) / not one, not any, none
n'importe qui, n'importe quel / anyone
n'importe quoi / anything

§6

on / people, one, they, you, we
  On dit qu'il va pleuvoir. / They say (that) it's going to rain.

Tip	*On* can also be understood as *nous*:
	Qu'est-ce qu'on fait demain? / What are we doing tomorrow? What shall we do tomorrow?

personne / no one, nobody
plusieurs / several
  J'en ai plusieurs. / I have several (of them).
quelque chose / something
quelqu'un (quelqu'une) / someone, somebody
quelques-uns (quelques-unes) / some, a few
quiconque / whoever, whosoever
soi / oneself
  On est chez soi dans cet hôtel. / People feel at home in this hotel.
tout / all, everything
  Tout est bien qui finit bien. / All is well that ends well.

§6.1–10 Interrogative Pronouns

Referring to Persons

• As subject of a verb:
  Qui est à l'appareil? / Who is on the phone?
  Qui est-ce qui est à l'appareil? / Who is on the phone?
  Lequel des deux garçons arrive? / Which (one) of the two boys is arriving?
  Laquelle des deux jeunes filles est ici? / Which (one) of the two girls is here?

• As direct object of a verb:
  Qui aimez-vous? / Whom do you love?
  Qui est-ce que vous aimez? / Whom do you love?
  Lequel de ces deux garçons aimez-vous? / Which (one) of these two boys do you love?
  Laquelle de ces deux jeunes filles aimez-vous? / Which (one) of these two girls do you love?

• As object of a preposition:

Avec qui allez-vous au cinéma? / With whom are you going to the movies?

A qui parlez-vous au téléphone? / To whom are you talking on the telephone?

Note that when the interrogative pronouns *lequel (laquelle)*, *lesquels (lesquelles)* are objects of the prepositions *à* or *de*, their forms are:

Singular	Plural
auquel (à laquelle)	*auxquels (auxquelles)*
duquel (de laquelle)	*desquels (desquelles)*

Auquel de ces deux garçons parlez-vous? / To which (one) of these two boys are you talking?

A laquelle de ces deux jeunes filles parlez-vous? / To which (one) of these two girls are you talking?

Auxquels de ces hommes parlez-vous? / To which (ones) of these men do you talk?

Auxquelles de ces femmes parlez-vous? / To which (ones) of these women are you talking?

Duquel de ces deux garçons parlez-vous? / About which (one) of these two boys are you talking?

Referring to Things

• As subject of a verb:

Qu'est-ce qui est arrivé? / What arrived? OR What happened?

Qu'est-ce qui s'est passé? / What happened?

Tip	***Une devinette avec qu'est-ce qui***

Qu'est-ce qui vous appartient et dont les autres se servent souvent? / What belongs to you that others use often?

votre nom / your name

Laquelle de ces deux voitures marche bien? / Which (one) of these two cars runs well?

Lesquels de tous ces trains sont modernes? / Which (ones) of all these trains are modern?

§6

- As direct object of a verb:

    Que faites-vous? / What are you doing?

    Qu'a-t-elle? / What does she have? OR What's the matter with her?

    Qu'est-ce que vous faites? / What are you doing?

    Laquelle de ces voitures préférez-vous? / Which (one) of these cars do you prefer?

- As object of a preposition:

    Avec quoi écrivez-vous? / With what are you writing?

    A quoi pensez-vous? / Of what are you thinking? OR What are you thinking of?

    De quoi parlez-vous? / What are you talking about? OR About what are you talking?

§6.1–11 Possessive Pronouns

MASCULINE			
Singular		**Plural**	
le mien	mine	*les miens*	mine
le tien	yours (familiar)	*les tiens*	yours (familiar)
le sien	his, hers, its	*les siens*	his, hers, its
le nôtre	ours	*les nôtres*	ours
le vôtre	yours	*les vôtres*	yours
le leur	theirs	*les leurs*	theirs
FEMININE			
Singular		**Plural**	
la mienne	mine	*les miennes*	mine
la tienne	yours (familiar)	*les tiennes*	yours (familiar)
la sienne	his, hers, its	*les siennes*	his, hers, its
la nôtre	ours	*les nôtres*	ours
la vôtre	yours	*les vôtres*	yours
la leur	theirs	*les leurs*	theirs

- A possessive pronoun takes the place of a possessive adjective + noun.

  mon livre / my book; *le mien* / mine.

- A possessive pronoun agrees in gender and number with what it is replacing.

  son livre / his (her) book; *le sien* / his (hers).

- When the definite articles *le* and *les* are preceded by the prepositions *à* and *de*, they combine as follows: *au mien, aux miens, du mien, des miens*.

  Paul me parle de ses parents et je lui parle des miens. / Paul is talking to me about his parents and I am talking to him about mine.

  Je préfère ma voiture à la tienne. / I prefer my car to yours.

- Possessive pronouns are used with *être* to emphasize a distinction.

  Ce livre-ci est le mien et celui-là est le tien. / This book is mine and that one is yours.

- If no distinction is made as to who owns what, use *être* + *à* + disjunctive pronoun. (§6.1–7)

  Ce livre est à lui. / This book is his.

- Instead of using the possessive pronouns in French, we say "one of my friends," "one of my books," etc.

  un de mes amis / a friend of mine; *un de mes livres* / a book of mine

  une de ses amies / a girlfriend of his (hers)

  un de nos amis / a friend of ours

§6

§6.1–12 Reflexive Pronouns

- The reflexive pronouns, which are used with reflexive verbs, are *me, te, se, nous,* and *vous.*
- The corresponding English pronouns are: myself, yourself, herself, himself, oneself, itself, ourselves, yourselves, themselves.
- To form the present tense of a reflexive verb in a simple affirmative sentence, put the reflexive pronoun in front of the verb.

  Je me lave. / I wash myself.

- A reflexive verb expresses an action that turns back upon the subject.

  Jacqueline se lave tous les jours. / Jacqueline washes herself every day.

 You must be careful to use the appropriate reflexive pronoun—the one that matches the subject pronoun. You already know the subject pronouns, but here they are again, beside the reflexive pronouns.

Person	Singular	Plural
1st	*je me lave*	*nous nous lavons*
2nd	*tu te laves*	*vous vous lavez*
3rd	⎧ *il se lave* ⎨ *elle se lave* ⎩ *on se lave*	⎧ *ils se lavent* ⎨ *elles se lavent*

Tip To get a picture of what the word order is when you have more than one pronoun of any kind in a sentence, see Order of Elements in French Sentences, §11.

§6.1–13 Relative Pronouns

Tip

A *relative pronoun* is a word that refers to an antecedent. An *antecedent* is something that comes before something; it can be a word, a phrase, or a clause that is replaced by a pronoun or some other substitute. For example, in the sentence "Is it Mary who did that?" "who" is the relative pronoun and "Mary" is the antecedent. Another example: "It seems to me that you are wrong, which is what I had suspected all along." The relative pronoun is "which" and the antecedent is the clause, "that you are wrong."

Some common relative pronouns are:

- *dont* / of whom, of which, whose, whom, which
  Voici le livre dont j'ai besoin. / Here is the book (that) I need.
  Monsieur Béry, dont le fils est avocat, est maintenant en France. / Mr. Béry, whose son is a lawyer, is now in France.

Tip

Remember that the relative pronoun *dont* replaces *de* in certain expressions that contain *de*: *avoir besoin de* / to need; *parler de* / to talk about; *rêver de* / to dream about.

- *ce dont* / what, of which, that of which
  Je ne trouve pas ce dont j'ai besoin. / I don't find what I need.
  Ce dont vous parlez est absurde. / What you are talking about is absurd.

- *ce que (ce qu')* / what, that which
  Comprenez-vous ce que je vous dis? / Do you understand what I am telling you?
  Comprenez-vous ce qu'elle vous dit? / Do you understand what she is saying to you?
  Je comprends ce que vous dites et je comprends ce qu'elle dit. / I understand what you are saying and I understand what she is saying.

§6

• *ce qui* / what, that which
> *Ce qui est vrai est vrai.* / What is true is true.
> *Je ne sais pas ce qui s'est passé.* / I don't know what happened.

Note that *ce qui* is a subject.

• *lequel* (in all its forms) / which

As a relative pronoun, *lequel* (in its various forms) is used as object of a preposition referring to things.
> *Donnez-moi un autre morceau de papier sur lequel je puisse écrire mon adresse.* / Give me another piece of paper on which I can write my address.

• *où* / where, in which, on which, when
> *Aimez-vous la salle à manger où nous mangeons?* / Do you like the dining room where we eat?
> *Je vais ouvrir le tiroir où j'ai mis l'argent.* / I am going to open the drawer where I put the money.
> *Il faisait beau le jour où elle est née.* / The weather was nice the day (when) she was born.

• *que* or *qu'* / whom, which, that
> *Le garçon que vous voyez là-bas est mon meilleur ami.* / The boy (whom) you see over there is my best friend.
> *La composition qu'elle a écrite est excellente.* / The composition (that) she wrote is excellent.

(Note the feminine agreement of *écrite* with *la composition* because the relative pronoun *que* (*qu'*) precedes the verb.) See §22, Agreement of Past Participle with its Preceding Direct Object.

| Tip | Note that the relative pronoun *que* (whom, which, or that) must be used in French but in English it is not always stated. |

• *qui* / who, whom, which, that
> *Connais-tu la jeune fille qui parle avec mon frère?* / Do you know the girl who is talking with my brother?
> *Avez-vous une bicyclette qui marche bien?* / Do you have a bicycle that (which) runs well?

§6.1–14 *C'est* + adjective + *à* + infinitive

C'est difficile à faire. / It is difficult to do.

Use this construction when what is being referred to *has already been mentioned.*

Examples:
Le devoir pour demain est difficile, n'est-ce pas? / The homework for tomorrow is difficult, isn't it?

Oui, c'est difficile à faire. / Yes, it [the homework] is difficult to do.

J'aimerais créer un site Web. / I would like to create a Web site.

C'est facile à faire! Je vais vous montrer. / It's easy to do! I'll show you.

§6.1–15 *Il est* + adjective + *de* + infinitive

Il est impossible de lire ce gros livre en une heure. / It is impossible to read this thick book within one hour.

Use this construction when the thing that is impossible, or difficult, or easy (or any adjective) to do is mentioned in the same sentence at the same time.

§6.1–16 Neuter Pronoun *le*

The word *le* is the masculine singular definite article. It is also the masculine singular direct object. *Le* is used as a neuter pronoun and functions as a direct object referring to an adjective, a phrase, a clause, or a complete statement. It is generally not translated into English, except to mean "it" or "so."

Janine est sportive, mais Henriette ne l'est pas. / Janine is athletic, but Henrietta isn't.

Moi, je crois qu'ils vont gagner le match, et vous? Je le crois aussi. / I think they are going to win the game, and you? I think so too.

§6

Tip

To get a picture of what the word order is when you have more than one pronoun of any kind in a sentence, see Order of Elements in French Sentences, §11.2 to §11.5.

Tip

Une devinette / a riddle

J'ai un chapeau, mais je n'ai pas de tête. Ne trouvez-vous pas que c'est bête? / I have a hat, but I don't have a head.
  Don't you think that's silly?

un champignon / a mushroom

§7.

Verbs,
Beginner, Intermediate, and
Advanced Levels

For a summary of the names of verb tenses and moods in French with English equivalents, see page 144.

§7.1 AGREEMENT

SUBJECT AND VERB

A subject and its corresponding verb form must agree in *person* (first, second, or third) and number (singular or plural).

Example:
Je vais au cinéma. / I'm going to the movies.

Tip A table of the French subject pronouns is in §6.1–1.

SUBJECT AND REFLEXIVE PRONOUN OF A REFLEXIVE VERB

A subject and reflexive pronoun must agree in person and number.

Example:
Je me lave tous les matins. / I wash myself every morning.

SUBJECT AND PAST PARTICIPLE OF AN *ÊTRE* VERB

The past participle of an *être* verb agrees with the subject in gender and number.

Elle est allée au cinéma. / She went to the movies. OR She has
gone to the movies.

Elles sont allées au cinéma. / They went to the movies. OR They
   have gone to the movies.

PRECEDING REFLEXIVE PRONOUN AND PAST PARTICIPLE OF A REFLEXIVE VERB

Elle s'est lavée. / She washed herself.
Elles se sont lavées. / They washed themselves.

However, there is *no* agreement made with the past participle of a reflexive verb if the reflexive pronoun serves as an
indirect object pronoun. In the following example, *se (s')* is the
indirect object; *les mains* is the direct object.

Elle s'est lavé les mains. / She washed her hands.
Elles se sont lavé les mains. / They washed their hands.

Note this:

Elles se sont regardées. / They looked at each other.

Here, the reflexive pronoun *se* serves as the direct object.
How do you know? There is no other obvious direct object
mentioned, so what they looked at was *se* (each other); of
course, you have to look at the subject to see what the
gender and number is of the reflexive pronoun *se* in the
sentence you are dealing with. The action of the verb is
reciprocal.

Remember that the verb *regarder* in French means "to
look at" in English; the preposition "at" is not expressed with
à in French; it is included in the verb—that is why we are
dealing with the reflexive pronoun as a direct object here,
not an indirect object pronoun.

This same sentence, *Elles se sont regardées*, might
also mean: "They looked at themselves." The principle of
agreement is still the same. If you mean to say "They
looked at each other," in order to avoid two meanings, add
l'une et l'autre. If more than two persons, add *les unes les
autres*.

And note:
Elles se sont parlé au téléphone. / They talked to each other on the telephone.

Here, the reflexive pronoun *se* is the indirect object because they spoke to each other; *parler à* is what you are dealing with here.

No agreement is made on a past participle with an indirect object. You must remember that.

PAST PARTICIPLE OF AN *AVOIR* VERB WITH A PRECEDING DIRECT OBJECT

Examples:

> *Je l'ai vue au concert.* / I saw her at the concert.

• There is agreement on the past participle *(vue)* because the preceding direct object is *la (l')*. Agreement is made in gender and number.

> *Aimez-vous les fleurs que je vous ai données?* / Do you like the flowers (that) I gave you?

• There is agreement on the past participle *(données)* of this *avoir* verb because there is a preceding direct object, *les fleurs*; the relative pronoun *que* refers to *les fleurs*. Since this direct object noun precedes the verb, the past participle must agree in gender and number. A preceding direct object, therefore, can be a pronoun or noun.

> *Quels films avez-vous vus?* / What films did you see?

• There is agreement on the past participle *(vus)* of this *avoir* verb because the preceding direct object, *films*, is a masculine plural noun.

> *Avez-vous mangé les pâtisseries?* / Did you eat the pastries?
> *Oui, je les ai mangées.* / Yes, I ate them.

- In the response to this question, there is agreement on the past participle *(mangées)* of this *avoir* verb because the preceding direct object, *les*, refers to *les pâtisseries*, a feminine plural noun.

> *J'en ai mangé assez.* / I ate enough (of them).

- There is no agreement on the past participle *(mangé)* of this *avoir* verb because the preceding direct object is, in this sentence, the pronoun *en*. We do not normally make an agreement with *en*, whether it precedes or follows. This is an exception. Review §6.1–5, *En*.

§7.2 PAST PARTICIPLE

REGULAR FORMATION

Infinitive	Type Ending	Drop	Add	Past Participle
donner	-er	-er	é	*donné*
finir	-ir	-ir	i	*fini*
vendre	-re	-re	u	*vendu*

COMMON IRREGULAR PAST PARTICIPLES

Infinitive	Past Participle
apprendre (to learn)	*appris*
asseoir (to seat; *s'asseoir* to sit down)	*assis*
avoir (to have)	*eu*
boire (to drink)	*bu*

Infinitive	Past Participle
comprendre (to understand)	*compris*
conduire (to lead, to drive)	*conduit*
connaître (to know)	*connu*
construire (to build)	*construit*
courir (to run)	*couru*
couvrir (to cover)	*couvert*
craindre (to fear)	*craint*
croire (to believe)	*cru*
devenir (to become)	*devenu*
devoir (to have to)	*dû*
dire (to say)	*dit*
écrire (to write)	*écrit*
être (to be)	*été*
faire (to do, to make)	*fait*
falloir (to be necessary)	*fallu*
lire (to read)	*lu*
mettre (to put)	*mis*
mourir (to die)	*mort*
naître (to be born)	*né*
offrir (to offer)	*offert*
ouvrir (to open)	*ouvert*
paraître (to seem)	*paru*
permettre (to permit)	*permis*
plaire (to please)	*plu*
pleuvoir (to rain)	*plu*
pouvoir (to be able)	*pu*
prendre (to take)	*pris*
promettre (to promise)	*promis*
recevoir (to receive)	*reçu*
revenir (to come back)	*revenu*
rire (to laugh)	*ri*
savoir (to know (how))	*su*

§7

Infinitive	Past Participle
suivre (to follow)	*suivi*
se taire (to be silent)	*tu*
tenir (to hold)	*tenu*
valoir (to be worth)	*valu*
venir (to come)	*venu*
vivre (to live)	*vécu*
voir (to see)	*vu*
vouloir (to want)	*voulu*

Examples:

Tout le monde a ri quand le clown a mis le feu à son pantalon. /
Everyone laughed when the clown set fire to his pants.

*Nous avons su que notre voisin a l'intention de déménager en
Belgique.* / We found out that our neighbor intends to move to
Belgium. (In the *passé composé*, *savoir* can mean "found out."
See §7.11, *Savoir*.)

§7.3 TYPES

§7.3–1 Helping Verbs (Auxiliary Verbs) *avoir* and *être*

Most verbs use **avoir** as the helping verb in the **passé
composé**. However, a number of verbs, in addition to
reflexive verbs, use **être** as the helping verb. The most
common ones are:

aller (to go)
arriver (to arrive)
descendre (to go down, come down)
devenir (to become)
entrer (to enter)
monter (to go up, come up)
mourir (to die)
naître (to be born)
partir (to leave)

passer (to go by, pass by)
rentrer (to go in again, to return home)
rester (to remain, stay)
retourner (to return, go back)
revenir (to come back)
sortir (to go out)
tomber (to fall)
venir (to come)

| Tip |

Most French verbs are conjugated with *avoir* to form a compound tense.
All reflexive verbs, such as *se laver,* are conjugated with *être*.

| Tip |

If you're having some trouble choosing your helping verb in the **passé composé,** just remember REM NAP, which is a tip to help you remember the French verbs we are dealing with in this unit.

Here is a way to break down the verbs that use **être** as a helping verb into smaller groups. Note the general similarity in the type of action described by the verbs in each group.

There are other ways to organize this. Some students use DR / MRS. VANDERTRAMP. However, that's pretty long. So, we're breaking the list down to something just as absurd but easier to use, because the verbs that use **être** are in smaller, more manageable groups. You can also use A DREAM or even SPAM AD. It's important that you be able to use the verbs while you're communicating, not just give a list. While you're studying, you may come up with a mnemonic device (memory tool) that works even better for you. If so, go ahead and use it!

Most of the verbs in the list are intransitive (taking no direct object) and use **être** as a helping verb. As you will see below, a few of them can sometimes be transitive (that is, they take a direct object), in which case you should use **avoir**. This will make more sense when you study **passer** and **sortir** (see below). Note the general similarity in the type of action described by the verbs in each group.

Retourner/Partir/Arriver (to return / to leave / to arrive)
Entrer-Rentrer/Sortir (to enter / to go back in / to go out)
Monter/Descendre/Tomber (to go up / to go down / to fall)

Naître/Mourir (to be born / to die)
Aller/Venir-Devenir-Revenir (to go / to come + some verbs based on **venir**)
Passer/Rester (to pass or to go by / to stay)

It's helpful to discuss the connections between the verbs in each of these groups. You may come up with a way that works better for you. This way of looking at the **être** verbs is simply a tool to help you organize your study. The best way to remember which verbs use **être** as a helping verb in the **passé composé** is to practice using them!

Remember that when the verb **être** is used as the helping verb, the past participle agrees in gender and number with the subject, just as you would make an adjective agree with the noun or pronoun that it modifies:

> **Il est grand.** / He is tall.
>
> **Ils sont grands.** / They are tall.
>
> **Elle est grande.** / She is tall.
>
> **Elles sont grandes.** / They are tall.

R
Retourner/Arriver/Partir

This group of verbs is used to talk about arrivals and departures (a bit like **naître** and **mourir**). They take the helping verb **être** in the **passé composé**.

Mes parents sont retournés. / My parents returned.

Madeleine est arrivée. / Madeleine arrived.

Francine est partie. / Francine left.

However, when **retourner** takes a direct object (meaning "to turn over" or "to turn around"), you should use **avoir** as the helping verb.

Quand Jean a retourné la pierre, il a trouvé ses clés. / When John turned over the stone, he found his keys.

E
Entrer-Rentrer/Sortir

Entrer and **sortir** are antonyms. **être** is the helping verb when you use **entrer** in the **passé composé**:

Nous sommes entrés par la porte principale. / We came in by the main door.

When it has no direct object, **rentrer** (to go in again, to return home) also uses **être** as its helping verb in the **passé composé**:

Anne et Marie sont rentrées à 23h. / Anne and Mary returned at 11 P.M.

But when **rentrer** takes a direct object, you should use **avoir** as the helping verb:

Frédéric a rentré le chat avant de fermer la porte. / Fred brought the cat inside before closing the door.

§7

Sortir is the antonym of **entrer**, and it also uses **être** as its helping verb in the **passé composé**.

Jeanne est sortie avec ses amis. / Jean went out with her friends.

However, if **sortir** takes a direct object, you should use **avoir** as the helping verb:

David a sorti son portefeuille pour chercher sa carte de crédit. / David took out his wallet to look for his credit card.

The direct object is **son portefeuille.** What did he take out? His wallet.

M
Monter/Descendre/Tomber

These three verbs are used to describe up or down movement. When **monter** and **descendre** are used intransitively (without a direct object), they use **être** as the helping verb.

Ariane est montée lentement. / Ariane went up slowly.

Ariane est descendue vite. / Ariane came down quickly.

When they are used transitively (with a direct object), these verbs take **avoir** as the helping verb.

Elle a monté l'escalier. (The direct object is **l'escalier**.) / She went up the stairs.

Elle a descendu la valise. (The direct object is **la valise.**) / She brought down the suitcase.

Tomber is almost always used intransitively and therefore usually takes **être** as its helping verb in the **passé composé**:

Elle est tombée dans l'escalier. / She fell down the stairs. (Lit.: She fell in the staircase.)

N
Naître/Mourir

Naître and its antonym, **mourir**, make a nice, inevitable pair. Both verbs take the helping verb **être** in the **passé composé**.

Ma tante est née en 1965. / My aunt was born in 1965.

Charles de Gaulle est mort en 1970. / Charles de Gaulle died in 1970.

A
Aller/Venir-Devenir-Revenir

Aller and **venir** are used to talk about opposite movements:

Marie est allée au supermarché. / Marie went to the supermarket.

Les Gosselin sont venus chez nous hier soir. / The Gosselins came to our home yesterday evening.

The verbs based on **venir** follow the same pattern in the **passé composé**.

Ma mère est devenue pédiatre pour aider les enfants. / My mother became a pediatrician to help children.

Est-ce que Pierre est revenu de l'école? / Has Peter come back from school?

P
Passer/Rester

Passer uses **être** as its auxiliary verb when it has no direct object (See §7.3–3):

Jean-Claude est passé au bureau de sa directrice. / Jean-Claude went by his director's office.

But **passer** uses **avoir** when it is used transitively (that is, with a direct object):

Elle m'a passé le sel. (The direct object is **le sel.** There is no feminine agreement on **passé.**) / She passed me the salt. OR She passed the salt to me.

Rester takes **être** as its auxiliary in the **passé composé.** While **passer** means to pass by, **rester** means "to stay." Well, they're not quite opposites.

Sabrina est restée à la maison parce qu'elle était malade. / Sabrina stayed at home because she was sick.

Tip	To see an **avoir** verb (**parler**) conjugated in all the tenses in French and English, see §7.6. To see an **être** verb (**venir**) conjugated in all the tenses in French and English, see §7.7.

§7.3–2 Transitive Verbs

A transitive verb is a verb that can take a direct object. It is transitive because the action passes over and directly affects something or someone in some way.

Je vois mon ami. / I see my friend. → *Je le vois.* / I see him.
Je ferme la fenêtre. / I am closing the window. → *Je la ferme.* / I'm closing it.

Tip	When the direct object of the verb is a pronoun, it is usually placed in front of the verb. The only time it is placed after the verb is in the affirmative imperative. To get an idea of the position of direct object pronouns see Order of Elements in French Sentences, §11.2 to §11.5.

§7.3–3 Intransitive Verbs

An intransitive verb is a verb that does not take a direct object. Such a verb is called intransitive because the action does not pass over and directly affect anyone or anything.

La maîtresse parle. / The teacher is talking.
Elle est partie tôt. / She left early.
Elles sont descendues vite. / They came down quickly.
Nous sommes montées lentement. / We went up slowly.

| Tip | Remember that verbs that normally take *être* as a helping verb in the *passé composé* take *avoir* if they are used transitively. In other words, the action is carried out on someone or something (see §22, Intransitive Verb and Transitive Verb). |

Example:
Elle a descendu la valise. / She brought down the suitcase.
(Transitive use of *descendre*.)

An intransitive verb can take an indirect object.
La maîtresse parle aux élèves. / The teacher is talking to the students.

Here the indirect object noun is *élèves* because it is preceded by *aux* / to the.
La maîtresse leur parle. / The teacher is talking to them.

Here the indirect object is the pronoun *leur*, meaning "to them."

§7.4 PRESENT PARTICIPLE

Regular Formation

The present participle is regularly formed in the following way: Take the *nous* form of the present indicative tense of the verb you have in mind, drop the first person plural ending *-ons*, and add *-ant*. That ending is equivalent to *-ing* in English.

Infinitive	Present Tense 1st Person Pl.	Drop -ons	Add -ant	Present Participle
finir / to finish	*nous finissons*	*finiss*	*ant*	*finissant*
manger / to eat	*nous mangeons*	*mange*	*ant*	*mangeant*
vendre / to sell	*nous vendons*	*vend*	*ant*	*vendant*
faire / to do; make	*nous faisons*	*fais*	*ant*	*faisant*
dire / to say; tell	*nous disons*	*dis*	*ant*	*disant*

Common Irregular Present Participles

Infinitive	Present Participle
avoir to have *être* to be *savoir* to know	*ayant* *étant* *sachant*

Tip If you're not sure which is a present participle and which is a past participle in French, associate the n in present with the *n* in the French ending *-ant* of a present participle.

```
        A
P R E S E N T
        T
```

En + Present Participle

The present participle in French is used primarily with the preposition *en*, meaning "on," "upon," "in," "while," "by."

en chantant / while singing
en finissant / upon finishing
en vendant / by selling
en mangeant / upon eating, while eating
en voyageant / by traveling
en ayant / on having
en étant / on being, upon being
en sachant / upon knowing

The present participle is sometimes used as an adjective.

un enfant amusant / an amusing child (boy)
une enfant amusante / an amusing child (girl)

§7.5 VERBS AND PREPOSITIONS

In this section you will learn what preposition goes with what verb.

Verb + *à* + Noun or Pronoun

* *assister à quelque chose (à une assemblée, à une réunion, à un spectacle, etc.)* / to attend or be present at (a gathering, a meeting, a theatrical presentation, etc.)
  Allez-vous assister à la conférence du professeur Godard? / Are you going to attend (be present at) Professor Godard's lecture?—*Oui, je vais y assister.* / Yes, I am going to attend it.

* *demander à quelqu'un* / to ask someone
  Demandez à la dame où s'arrête l'autobus. / Ask the lady where the bus stops.

* *désobéir à quelqu'un* / to disobey someone
  Ce chien ne désobéit jamais à son maître. / This dog never disobeys his master.
  Il ne lui désobéit jamais. / He never disobeys him.

* *être à quelqu'un* / to belong to someone
  Ce livre est à Victor. / This book belongs to Victor.

§7

- *faire attention à quelqu'un ou à quelque chose* / to pay attention to someone or to something

  Faites attention au professeur. / Pay attention to the professor.

- *s'intéresser à quelqu'un ou à quelque chose* / to be interested in someone or something

  Je m'intéresse aux sports. / I am interested in sports.

- *jouer à* / to play (a game or sport)

  Il aime bien jouer à la balle. / He likes to play ball.
  Elle aime bien jouer au tennis. / She likes to play tennis.

- *obéir à quelqu'un* / to obey someone
  Une personne honorable obéit à ses parents. / An honorable person obeys his (her) parents.

- *participer à quelque chose* / to participate in something

  Je participe aux sports. / I participate in sports.

- *penser à quelqu'un ou à quelque chose* / to think of (about) someone or something

  Je pense à mes amis. / I am thinking of my friends.
  Je pense à eux. / I am thinking of them.
  Je pense à mon travail. / I am thinking about my work.
  J'y pense. / I am thinking about it.

- *répondre à quelqu'un ou à quelque chose* / to answer someone or something

  J'ai répondu au professeur. / I answered the teacher.
  Je lui ai répondu. / I answered him.
  J'ai répondu à la lettre. / I answered the letter.
  J'y ai répondu. / I answered it.

- *ressembler à quelqu'un* / to resemble someone
  Il ressemble beaucoup à sa mère. / He resembles his mother a lot.

- *réussir à quelque chose* / to succeed in something
  réussir à un examen / to pass an examination
  Il a réussi à l'examen. / He passed the exam.

- *téléphoner à quelqu'un* / to telephone someone
  Marie a téléphoné à Paul. / Marie telephoned Paul.
  Elle lui a téléphoné. / She telephoned him.

Verb + *à* + Infinitive

- *aider à* / to help
  Roger aide son petit frère à faire son devoir de mathématiques. / Roger is helping his little brother to do his math homework.

- *s'amuser à* / to amuse oneself, enjoy, have fun
  Il y a des élèves qui s'amusent à mettre le professeur en colère. / There are pupils who enjoy making the teacher angry.

- *apprendre à* / to learn
  J'apprends à lire. / I am learning to read.

- *s'attendre à* / to expect
  Je m'attendais à trouver une salle de classe vide. / I was expecting to find an empty classroom.

- *avoir à* / to have to, to be obliged to (do something)
  J'ai mes devoirs à faire ce soir. / I have to do my homework tonight.

- *commencer à* / to begin
  Il commence à pleuvoir. / It is beginning to rain.

- *continuer à* / to continue
  Je continue à étudier le français. / I am continuing to study French.

- *décider quelqu'un à* / to persuade someone
  J'ai décidé mon père à me prêter quelques euros. / I persuaded my father to lend me a few euros.

- *se décider à* / to make up one's mind
  Il s'est décidé à l'épouser. / He made up his mind to marry her.

- *demander à* / to ask, request
  Elle demande à parler. / She asks to speak.

- *encourager à* / to encourage
  Je l'ai encouragé à suivre un cours de français. / I encouraged him to take a course in French.

- *enseigner à* / to teach
  Je vous enseigne à lire en français. / I am teaching you to read in French.

- *s'habituer à* / to get used (to)
    Je m'habitue à parler français couramment. / I am getting used to speaking French fluently.

- *hésiter à* / to hesitate
    J'hésite à répondre à sa lettre. / I hesitate to reply to her (his) letter.

- *inviter à* / to invite
    Monsieur et Madame Boivin ont invité les Béry à dîner chez eux. / Mr. and Mrs. Boivin invited the Bérys to have dinner at their house.

- *se mettre à* / to begin
    L'enfant se met à rire. / The child is beginning to laugh.

- *parvenir à* / to succeed
    Elle est parvenue à être docteur. / She succeeded in becoming a doctor.

- *se plaire à* / to take pleasure in
    Il se plaît à taquiner ses amis. / He takes pleasure in teasing his friends.

- *recommencer à* / to begin again
    Il recommence à pleuvoir. / It is beginning to rain again.

- *réussir à* / to succeed in
    Henri a réussi à me convaincre. / Henry succeeded in convincing me.

- *songer à* / to dream; to think
    Elle songe à diriger une entreprise. / She is dreaming of running a business.

- *tenir à* / to insist, be anxious
    Je tiens absolument à voir mon enfant immédiatement. / I am very anxious to see my child immediately.

Verb + *de* + Noun

- *s'agir de* / to be a question of, a matter of
    Il s'agit de l'amour. / It is a matter of love.

- *s'approcher de* / to approach
  La dame s'approche de la porte et elle l'ouvre. / The lady
  approaches the door and opens it.

- *changer de* / to change
  Je dois changer de train à Paris. / I have to change trains in Paris.

- *se douter de* / to suspect
  Je me doute de ses opinions. / I suspect his (her) opinions.

- *féliciter de* / to congratulate on
  Je vous félicite de vos progrès. / I congratulate you on your progress.

- *jouer de* / to play (a musical instrument)
  Je sais jouer du piano. / I know how to play the piano.

- *manquer de* / to lack
  Cette personne manque de politesse. / This person lacks
  courtesy.

- *se méfier de* / to distrust, to mistrust, to beware of
  Je me méfie des personnes que je ne connais pas. / I distrust persons whom I do not know.

- *se moquer de* / to make fun of
  Les enfants aiment se moquer d'un singe. / Children like to make
  fun of a monkey.

- *s'occuper de* / to be busy with
  Madame Boulanger s'occupe de son mari infirme. / Mrs. Boulanger
  is busy with her disabled husband.
  Je m'occupe de mes affaires. / I mind my own business.
  Occupez-vous de vos affaires! / Mind your own business!

- *partir de* / to leave
  Il est parti de la maison à huit heures. / He left the house at
  eight o'clock.

- *se plaindre de* / to complain about
  Il se plaint toujours de son travail. / He always complains about his
  work.

§7

- *remercier de* / to thank
  Je vous remercie de votre bonté. / I thank you for your kindness.

Tip	(Use *remercier de* + an abstract noun or infinitive; *remercier pour* + a concrete object; e.g., *Je vous remercie pour le cadeau.* / I thank you for the present.)

- *se rendre compte de* / to realize, to be aware of
  Je me rends compte de la condition de cette personne. / I am aware of the condition of this person.

- *se servir de* / to employ, use, make use of
  Je me sers d'un stylo quand j'écris une lettre. / I use a pen when I write a letter.

- *se souvenir de* / to remember
  Oui, je me souviens de Gervaise. / Yes, I remember Gervaise.
  Je me souviens de lui. / I remember him.
  Je me souviens d'elle. / I remember her.
  Je me souviens de l'été passé. / I remember last summer.
  Je m'en souviens. / I remember it.

- *tenir de* / to take after (to resemble)
  Julie tient de sa mère. / Julie takes after her mother.

Verb + *de* + Infinitive

- *s'agir de* / to be a question of, a matter of (This verb is impersonal.)
  Il s'agit de faire les devoirs tous les jours. / It is a matter of doing the homework every day.

- *avoir peur de* / to be afraid of
  Le petit garçon a peur de traverser la rue seul. / The little boy is afraid of crossing the street alone.

- *cesser de* / to stop, cease
  Il a cessé de pleuvoir. / It has stopped raining.

- *craindre de* / to be afraid of, fear
  La petite fille craint de traverser la rue seule. / The little girl is afraid of crossing the street alone.

- *décider de* / to decide
  J'ai décidé de partir tout de suite. / I decided to leave
    immediately.

- *demander de* / to ask, request
  Je vous demande de parler. / I am asking you to speak.

| Tip | (Note that here the subjects are different: *I* am asking *you* to speak; but when the subjects are the same, use *demander à: Elle demande à parler.* / She is asking to speak.) |

- *se dépêcher de* / to hurry
  *Je me suis dépêché de venir chez vous pour vous dire quelque
    chose.* / I hurried to come to your place in order to tell me some-
    thing.

- *empêcher de* / to keep from, prevent
  Je vous empêche de sortir. / I prevent you from going out.

- essayer de / to try (When you conjugate a verb that ends
  in **-ayer,** you may change **y** to **i** in front of a mute **e.** You
  may also keep the **y.**)
  J'essaie d'ouvrir la porte mais je ne peux pas. / I'm trying to open
    the door but I can't.

- *féliciter de* / to congratulate
  On m'a félicité d'avoir gagné le prix. / I was congratulated on hav-
    ing won the prize.

- *finir de* / to finish
  J'ai fini de travailler sur cette composition. / I have finished
    working on this composition.

- *se hâter de* / to hurry
  Je me hâte de venir chez toi. / I am hurrying to come to your
    house.

- *offrir de* / to offer
  J'ai offert d'écrire une lettre pour elle. / I offered to write a letter for
    her.

- *oublier de* / to forget
  J'ai oublié de vous donner la monnaie. / I forgot to give you the
    change.

§7

- *persuader de* / to persuade
  J'ai persuadé mon père de me prêter quelques euros. /
    I persuaded my father to lend me a few euros.

- *prendre garde de* / to take care not to
  Prenez garde de tomber. / Be careful not to fall.

- *prier de* / to beg
  Je vous prie d'arrêter. / I beg you to stop.

 Je vous en prie. Literally, this means "I beg of you." It is a polite way of accepting a compliment or saying, "You're welcome."
Merci, monsieur. / Thank you, sir.
Je vous en prie, madame. / You're welcome, ma'am.

- *promettre de* / to promise
  J'ai promis de venir chez toi à huit heures. / I promised to come to your place at eight o'clock.

- *refuser de* / to refuse
  Je refuse de le croire. / I refuse to believe it.

- *regretter de* / to regret, be sorry
  Je regrette d'être obligé de vous dire cela. / I am sorry to be obliged to tell you that.

- *remercier de* / to thank
  Je vous remercie d'être venu si vite. / I thank you for coming (having come) so quickly. (Use *remercier de* + infinitive or + abstract noun. Use *remercier pour* + concrete object.)

- *se souvenir de* / to remember
  Tu vois? Je me suis souvenu de venir chez toi. / You see? I remembered to come to your house.

- *tâcher de* / to try
  Tâche de finir tes devoirs avant de sortir. / Try to finish your homework before going out.

- *venir de* / to have just (done something)
  Je viens de manger. / I have just eaten. (I just ate.)

Verb + *à* + Noun + *de* + Infinitive

The model to follow is: *J'ai conseillé à Robert de suivre un cours de français.* / I advised Robert to take a course in French.

* *conseiller à* / to advise

  J'ai conseillé à Jeanne de se marier. / I advised Joan to get married.

* *défendre à* / to forbid

  Mon père défend à mon frère de fumer. / My father forbids my brother to smoke.

* *demander à* / to ask, request

  J'ai demandé à Marie de venir. / I asked Mary to come.

* *dire à* / to say, to tell

  J'ai dit à Charles de venir. / I told Charles to come.

* *interdire à* / to forbid

  Mon père interdit à mon frère de fumer. / My father forbids my brother to smoke.

* *permettre à* / to permit

  J'ai permis à l'étudiant de partir quelques minutes avant la fin de la classe. / I permitted the student to leave a few minutes before the end of class.

* *promettre à* / to promise

  J'ai promis à mon ami d'arriver à l'heure. / I promised my friend to arrive on time.

* *téléphoner à* / to telephone

  J'ai téléphoné à Marcel de venir me voir. / I phoned Marcel to come to see me.

Verb + Other Prepositions

* *commencer par* + infinitive / to begin by + present participle

  La présidente a commencé par discuter des problèmes de la société. / The president began by discussing problems in society.

- *s'entendre avec quelqu'un* / to get along with someone
  Jean s'entend avec Christophe. / John gets along with Christopher.

- *entrer dans* + noun / to enter, go in
  Elle est entrée dans le restaurant. / She went into the restaurant.

- *insister pour* + infinitive / to insist on, upon
  J'insiste pour obtenir tous mes droits. / I insist on obtaining all
    my rights.

- *se marier avec quelqu'un* / to marry someone
  Elle va se marier avec lui. / She is going to marry him.

- *se mettre en colère* / to become angry, upset
  Monsieur Leduc se met en colère facilement. / Mr. Leduc gets
    angry easily.

- *se mettre en route* / to start out, set out
  Ils se sont mis en route dès l'aube. / They started out at dawn.

- *remercier pour* + a concrete noun / to thank for
  Je vous remercie pour le joli cadeau. / I thank you for the pretty
    present. (Remember to use *remercier de* + an abstract noun or +
    infinitive: *Je vous remercie de votre bonté.* / I thank you for your
    kindness. *Je vous remercie d'être venue si vite.* / I thank you for
    coming so quickly.)

Verb + no preposition + Infinitive

The following verbs take *no* preposition and are followed directly by the infinitive.

- *adorer* / to adore, love
  Madame Morin adore naviguer sur Internet. / Mrs. Morin loves to
    surf the Internet.

- *aimer* / to like
  J'aime lire. / I like to read.

- *aimer mieux* / to prefer
  J'aime mieux rester ici. / I prefer to stay here.

- *aller* / to go
  Je vais faire mes devoirs. / I am going to do my homework.

 Tip For the use of **aller** + inf. as a near future tense, see §7.8–4, page 92.

- *compter* / to intend
  Je compte aller en France l'été prochain. / I intend to go to France next summer.

- *croire* / to believe
  Il croit être innocent. / He believes he is innocent.

- *désirer* / to desire, wish
  Je désire prendre une tasse de café. / I wish to have a cup of coffee.

- *devoir* / to have to, ought to
  Je dois faire mes devoirs avant de sortir. / I have to do my homework before going out.

- *écouter* / to listen to
  J'écoute chanter les enfants. / I am listening to the children singing.

- *entendre* / to hear
  J'entends chanter les enfants. / I hear the children singing.

- *espérer* / to hope
  J'espère aller en France. / I hope to go to France.

- *faire* / to cause; to make; to have something done by someone
  Le professeur fait travailler les élèves dans la salle de classe. / The teacher has the pupils work in the classroom.

falloir / to be necessary
  Il faut être honnête. / One must be honest.

laisser / to let, allow
  Je vous laisse partir. / I am letting you go.

paraître / to appear, seem
  Elle paraît être capable. / She appears to be capable.

penser / to think, plan, intend
  Je pense aller à Paris. / I intend to go to Paris.

pouvoir / to be able, can
   Je peux marcher mieux maintenant. / I can walk better now.

préférer / to prefer
   Je préfère manger maintenant. / I prefer to eat now.

regarder / to look at
   Je regarde voler les oiseaux. / I am looking at the birds flying.

savoir / to know, know how
   Je sais nager. / I know how to swim.

valoir mieux / to be better
   Il vaut mieux être honnête. / It is better to be honest.

vouloir / to want
   Je veux venir chez vous. / I want to come to your house.

Verbs That Do Not Require a Preposition

| Tip |

In English, there are many "phrasal verbs" that add a preposition or adverb in order to take on a different shade of meaning. However, we often do not need a preposition or adverb to express the same thought in French: to look for / *chercher,* to look at / *regarder.*

- *attendre* / to wait for
   J'attends l'autobus depuis vingt minutes. / I have been waiting for the bus for twenty minutes.

- *chercher* / to look for
   Je cherche mon livre. / I'm looking for my book.

- *demander* / to ask for
   Je demande une réponse. / I am asking for a reply.

- *écouter* / to listen to
   J'écoute la musique. / I am listening to the music.
   J'écoute le professeur. / I am listening to the teacher.

- *envoyer chercher* / to send for
   J'ai envoyé chercher le docteur. / I sent for the doctor.

- *essayer* / to try on
  Elle a essayé une jolie robe. / She tried on a pretty dress.

- *mettre* / to put on
  Elle a mis la robe rouge. / She put on the red dress.

- *payer* / to pay for
  J'ai payé le dîner. / I paid for the dinner.

- *pleurer* / to cry about, cry over
  Elle pleure la perte de son petit chien. / She is crying over the loss of her little dog.

- *regarder* / to look at
  Je regarde le ciel. / I am looking at the sky.

§7.6 COMPLETE CONJUGATION OF AN *AVOIR* VERB

Present participle: *parlant*/ talking, speaking; Past participle: *parlé*/ talked, spoken; Infinitive: *parler*/ to talk, to speak

Present indicative	*je parle, tu parles, il (elle, on) parle; nous parlons, vous parlez, ils (elles) parlent*

I talk, you talk, he (she, it, one) talks; we talk, you talk, they talk

OR

I do talk, etc.

OR

I am talking, etc.

Imperfect indicative	*je parlais, tu parlais, il (elle, on) parlait; nous parlions, vous parliez, ils (elles) parlaient*

I was talking, you were talking, he (she, it, one) was talking; we were talking, you were talking, they were talking

OR

I used to talk, etc.

OR

I talked, etc.

Simple past (Past definite)	*je parlai, tu parlas, il (elle, on) parla; nous parlâmes, vous parlâtes, ils (elles) parlèrent*

I talked, you talked, he (she, it, one) talked; we talked, you talked, they talked

OR

I did talk, etc.

Future	*je parlerai, tu parleras, il (elle, on) parlera; nous parlerons, vous parlerez, ils (elles) parleront*

I shall talk, you will talk, he (she, it, one) will talk; we shall talk, you will talk, they will talk

Conditional present	*je parlerais, tu parlerais, il (elle, on) parlerait; nous parlerions, vous parleriez, ils (elles) parleraient*

I would talk, you would talk, he (she, it, one) would talk; we would talk, you would talk, they would talk

Present subjunctive	*que je parle, que tu parles, qu'il (qu'elle, qu'on) parle; que nous parlions, que vous parliez, qu'ils (qu'elles) parlent*

that I may talk, that you may talk, that he (she, it, one) may talk; that we may talk, that you may talk, that they may talk

*Imperfect subjunctive	*que je parlasse, que tu parlasses, qu'il (qu'elle, qu'on) parlât; que nous parlassions, que vous parlassiez, qu'ils (qu'elles) parlassent*

* The imperfect subjunctive is not used much these days. However, you will see it when you read literature.

that I might talk, that you might talk, that he (she, it, one) might talk; that we might talk, that you might talk, that they might talk

Passé composé (Past indefinite)
j'ai parlé, tu as parlé, il (elle, on) a parlé; nous avons parlé, vous avez parlé, ils (elles) ont parlé

I talked, you talked, he (she, it, one) talked; we talked, you talked, they talked

OR

I have talked, you have talked, he (she, it, one) has talked; we have talked, you have talked, they have talked

OR

I did talk, you did talk, he (she, it, one) did talk; we did talk, you did talk, they did talk

Pluperfect indicative
j'avais parlé, tu avais parlé, il (elle, on) avait parlé; nous avions parlé, vous aviez parlé, ils (elles) avaient parlé

I had talked, you had talked, he (she, it, one) had talked; we had talked, you had talked, they had talked

Past anterior
j'eus parlé, tu eus parlé, il (elle, on) eut parlé; nous eûmes parlé, vous eûtes parlé, ils (elles) eurent parlé

I had talked, you had talked, he (she, it, one) had talked; we had talked, you had talked, they had talked

Future perfect
j'aurai parlé, tu auras parlé, il (elle, on) aura parlé; nous aurons parlé, vous aurez parlé, ils (elles) auront parlé

I shall have talked, you will have talked, he (she, it, one) will have talked; we shall have talked, you will have talked, they will have talked

§7

Conditional perfect	*j'aurais parlé, tu aurais parlé, il (elle, on) aurait parlé; nous aurions parlé, vous auriez parlé, ils (elles) auraient parlé*
	I would have talked, you would have talked, he (she, it, one) would have talked; we would have talked, you would have talked, they would have talked
Past subjunctive	*que j'aie parlé, que tu aies parlé, qu'il (qu'elle, qu'on) ait parlé; que nous ayons parlé, que vous ayez parlé, qu'ils (qu'elles) aient parlé*
	that I may have talked, that you may have talked, that he (she, it, one) may have talked; that we may have talked, that you may have talked, that they may have talked
*Pluperfect subjunctive	*que j'eusse parlé, que tu eusses parlé, qu'il (qu'elle, qu'on) eût parlé; que nous eussions parlé, que vous eussiez parlé, qu'ils (qu'elles) eussent parlé*
	that I might have talked, that you might have talked, that he (she, it, one) might have talked; that we might have talked, that you might have talked, that they might have talked
Imperative	*parle, parlons, parlez*
	talk, let's talk, talk

---

* The pluperfect subjunctive is not used much these days. However, you may see it when reading literature.

§7.7 COMPLETE CONJUGATION OF AN *ÊTRE* VERB

Present participle: *venant*/ coming; Past participle; *venu*/ come; Infinitive: *venir*/ to come

Present indicative	*je viens, tu viens, il (elle, on) vient; nous venons, vous venez, ils (elles) viennent*

I come, you come, he (she, it, one) comes; we come, you come, they come

OR

I do come, etc.

OR

I am coming, etc.

Imperfect indicative	*je venais, tu venais, il (elle, on) venait; nous venions, vous veniez, ils (elles) venaient*

I was coming, you were coming, he (she, it, one) was coming; we were coming, you were coming, they were coming

OR

I used to come, etc.

OR

I came, etc.

Simple past (Past definite)	*je vins, tu vins, il (elle, on) vint; nous vînmes, vous vîntes, ils (elles) vinrent*

I came, you came, he (she, it, one) came; we came, you came, they came

OR

I did come, etc.

Future	*je viendrai, tu viendras, il (elle, on) viendra; nous viendrons, vous viendrez, ils (elles) viendront*

§7

I shall come, you will come, he (she, it, one) will come; we shall come, you will come, they will come

Conditional present	*je viendrais, tu viendrais, il (elle, on) viendrait; nous viendrions, vous viendriez, ils (elles) viendraient*

I would come, you would come, he (she, it, one) would come; we would come, you would come, they would come

Present subjunctive	*que je vienne, que tu viennes, qu'il (qu'elle, qu'on) vienne; que nous venions, que vous veniez, qu'ils (qu'elles) viennent*

that I may come, that you may come, that he (she, it, one) may come; that we may come, that you may come, that they may come

Imperfect subjunctive	*que je vinsse, que tu vinsses, qu'il (qu'elle, qu'on) vînt; que nous vinssions, que vous vinssiez, qu'ils (qu'elles) vinssent*

that I might come, that you might come, that he (she, it, one) might come; that we might come, that you might come, that they might come

Passé composé (Past indefinite)	*je suis venu(e), tu es venu(e), il (on) est venu, elle est venue; nous sommes venu(e)s, vous êtes venu(e)(s), ils sont venus, elles sont venues*

I came, you came, he (she, it one) came; we came, you came, they came

OR

I have come, etc.

OR

I did come, etc.

Pluperfect indicative	*j'étais venu(e), tu étais venu(e), il, on était venu, elle était venue; nous étions venu(e)s, vous étiez venu(e)(s), ils étaient venus, elles étaient venues*

I had come, you had come, he (she, it, one) had come; we had come, you had come, they had come

Past anterior	*je fus venu(e), tu fus venu(e), il (on) fut venu, elle fut venue; nous fûmes venu(e)s, vous fûtes venu(e)(s), ils furent venus, elles furent venues*

I had come, you had come, he (she, it, one) had come; we had come, you had come, they had come

Future perfect	*je serai venu(e), tu seras venu(e), il (on) sera venu, elle sera venue; nous serons venu(e)s, vous serez venu(e)(s), ils seront venus, elles seront venues*

I shall have come, you will have come, he (she, it, one) will have come; we shall have come, you will have come, they will have come

Conditional perfect	*je serais venu(e), tu serais venu(e), il (on) serait venu, elle serait venue; nous serions venu(e)s, vous seriez venu(e)(s), ils seraient venus, elles seraient venues*

I would have come, you would have come, he (she, it, one) would have come; we would have come, you would have come, they would have come

§7

Past subjunctive	*que je sois venu(e), que tu sois venu(e), qu'il (on) soit venu, qu'elle soit venue; que nous soyons venu(e)s, que vous soyez venu(e)(s), qu'ils soient venus, qu'elles soient venues*
	that I may have come, that you may have come, that he (she, it, one) may have come; that we may have come, that you may have come, that they may have come
Pluperfect subjunctive	*que je fusse venu(e), que tu fusses venu(e), qu'il (qu'on) fût venu, qu'elle fût venue; que nous fussions venu(e)s, que vous fussiez venu(e)(s), qu'ils fussent venus, qu'elles fussent venues*
	that I might have come, that you might have come, that he (she, it, one) might have come; that we might have come, that you might have come, that they might have come
Imperative	*viens, venons, venez*
	come, let's come, come

§7.8 TENSES AND MOODS

Beginner Level

§7.8–1 Present Indicative Tense

The *present indicative* is the most frequently used tense in French and English. It indicates:

- An action or a state of being at the present time.
  Je vais à l'école maintenant. / I am going to school now.
  Je pense; donc, je suis. / I think; therefore, I am.

- Habitual action.
  Je vais à la bibliothèque tous les jours. / I go to the library every day.

- A general truth, something that is permanently true.
  Deux et deux font quatre. / Two and two are four.
  Voir c'est croire. / Seeing is believing.

- Vividness when talking or writing about past events.
  Marie-Antoinette est condamnée à mort. Elle monte dans la charrette et elle est en route pour la guillotine. / Marie-Antoinette is condemned to die. She gets into the cart and she is on her way to the guillotine.

- A near future.
  Il arrive demain. / He arrives tomorrow.

- An action or state of being that occurred in the past and continues up to the present. In English, this tense is the present perfect, which is formed with the present tense of "to have" plus the past participle of the verb you are using.
  Je suis ici depuis dix minutes. / I have been here for ten minutes. (I am still here at present.)

  This tense is regularly formed as follows:

Regular -er verb formation:

Drop the *-er* ending of an infinitive like *parler*, and add *-e, -es, -e; -ons, -ez, -ent*.

You then get:
je parle, tu parles, il (elle, on) parle; nous parlons, vous parlez, ils (elles) parlent

---

Regular -ir verb formation:

Drop the *-ir* ending of an infinitive like *finir*, and add *-is, -is, -it; -issons, -issez, -issent*.

You then get:
je finis, tu finis, il (elle, on) finit; nous finissons, vous finissez, ils (elles) finissent

§7

> **Regular -re verb formation:**
> Drop the *-re* ending of an infinitive like *vendre*, and add *-s,
> -s, —; -ons, -ez, -ent.*
>
> You then get:
> *je vends, tu vends, il (elle, on) vend; nous vendons, vous
> vendez, ils (elles) vendent*

For the present tense of *avoir* and *être*, see §7.19.

§7.8–2 Imperfect Indicative Tense

The *imperfect indicative* is a past tense. It is used to indicate:

• An action that was going on in the past at the same time as
another action.

> *Il lisait pendant que j'écrivais.* / He was reading while I was
> writing.

• An action that was going on in the past when another action
occurred.

> *Il lisait quand je suis entré.* / He was reading when I came in.

• An action that was performed habitually in the past.

> *Nous allions à la plage tous les jours.* / We used to go to the
> beach every day.

• A description of a mental or physical condition in the past.

> (mental) *Il était triste quand je l'ai vu.* / He was sad when
> I saw him.
> (physical) *Quand ma mère était jeune, elle était belle.* /
> When my mother was young, she was beautiful.

- An action or state of being that occurred in the past and lasted for a certain length of time prior to another past action.

> *J'attendais l'autobus depuis dix minutes quand il est arrivé.* / I had been waiting for the bus for ten minutes when it arrived.

Imperfect tense formation:

This tense is regularly formed as follows:

For *-er*, *-ir*, and *-re* verbs, take the "*nous*" form in the present indicative tense of the verb you have in mind, drop the first person plural ending (*-ons*), and add the endings *-ais, -ais, -ait; -ions, -iez, -aient.*

| Tip | The vowel *i* is in each of the six endings and *i* is the first letter of the *imperfect* tense. |

| Tip | Note that verbs that end in *-ier* have *ii* in the imperfect tense of the *nous* and *vous* forms. This can be confusing for some beginning students, but it is correct. |

Example:
Nous étudiions. / We were studying.

For the imperfect indicative of *avoir* and *être*, see §7.19.

§7.8–3 Simple Past Tense (Past Definite)

This past tense is not ordinarily used in conversational French or in informal writing. It is a literary tense—used in formal writing, such as history and literature. The French name of this tense is *le passé simple*. For a summary of the names of verb tenses and moods in French with English equivalents, see page 144.

Simple past tense formation:

The simple past tense is regularly formed as follows:
For all -*er* verbs, drop the -*er* of the infinitive and add
-*ai, -as, -a; -âmes, -âtes, -èrent*.
For regular -*ir* and -*re* verbs, drop the ending of the
infinitive and add the endings -*is, -is, it; -îmes, -îtes, -irent*.

Il alla en Afrique. / He went to Africa.

Il voyagea en Amérique. / He traveled to America.

Elle fut heureuse. / She was happy.

Elle eut un grand bonheur. / She had great happiness.

For the simple past (past definite) of *avoir* and *être*,
see §7.19.

§7.8–4 Future Tense

In French and English the *future* tense is used to express an
action or a state of being which will take place at some time
in the future.

*J'irai en France l'été prochain. / I will go to France next summer.

J'y penserai. / I will think about it.

Je partirai dès qu'il arrivera. / I will leave as soon as he arrives.

Je te dirai tout quand tu seras ici. / I will tell you all when you are
here.

| Tip |

*Instead of using the future tense of **aller** (as in
j'irai), it is correct to use **aller** in the present
tense + infinitive, as in Je vais aller *en France
l'été prochain.* / I am going to go to France next
summer.

If the action of the verb you are using is not past or
present and if future time is implied, the future tense is used
when the clause begins with the following conjunctions:
aussitôt que / as soon as, *dès que* / as soon as, *quand* /
when, *lorsque* / when, and *tant que* / as long as.

Future tense formation:

This tense is regularly formed as follows:
Add the following endings to the whole infinitive: *-ai, -as,
-a, -ons, -ez, -ont*. For *-re* verbs you must drop the *e* in
-re before you add the future endings.

| Tip | Note the similarity between the future tense endings and the present tense forms of *avoir* (*ai, as, a; avons, avez, ont*). |

For the future of *avoir* and *être*, see §7.19.

§7.8–5 Conditional Present Tense

The conditional mood is used in French and English to
express:

• An action that you would do if something else were
possible.

Je ferais le travail si j'en avais le temps. / I would do the work if
I had the time.

See also §7.10 for a summary of **si** (if) clauses, on page 103.

• A conditional desire. You should use this tense to be
polite—for example, when ordering in a restaurant.

J'aimerais du thé. / I would like some tea.
Je voudrais du café. / I would like some coffee.

• An obligation or duty.

Je devrais étudier pour l'examen. / I should study for the
examination.

§7

> **Conditional tense formation:**
>
> The present conditional is regularly formed as follows:
>
> Add the following endings to the whole infinitive: *-ais, -ais, -ait; -ions, -iez, -aient*. For *-re* verbs you must drop the *e* in *-re* before you add the conditional endings. Note that these endings are the same ones you use to form regularly the imperfect indicative. For the conditional of *avoir* and *être*, see §7.19.

Intermediate Level

§7.8–6 Present Subjunctive Tense

The subjunctive mood is used in French much more than in English. It is used in the following ways:

- After a verb that expresses some kind of insistence, preference, or suggestion.

    Je préfère qu'il fasse le travail maintenant. / I prefer that he do the work now.

    Le juge exige qu'il soit puni. / The judge demands that he be punished.

- After a verb that expresses doubt, fear, joy, sorrow, or some other emotion.

    Sylvie doute qu'il vienne. / Sylvia doubts that he is coming.

    Je suis heureux qu'il vienne. / I'm happy that he is coming.

    Je regrette qu'il soit malade. / I'm sorry that he is sick.

- After certain conjunctions.

    Elle partira à moins qu'il ne vienne. / She will leave unless he comes.

    Je resterai jusqu'à ce qu'il vienne. / I will stay until he comes.

    Quoiqu'elle soit belle, il ne l'aime pas. / Although she is beautiful, he does not love her.

    Le professeur l'explique pour qu'elle comprenne. / The teacher is explaining it so that she may understand.

• After certain impersonal expressions that show a need, a
doubt, a possibility, or an impossibility.

Il est urgent qu'il vienne. / It is urgent that he come.

Il vaut mieux qu'il vienne. / It is better that he come.

Il est possible qu'il vienne. / It is possible that he will come.

Il est douteux qu'il vienne. / It is doubtful that he will come.

For more verbs and expressions that require the subjunctive
mood, see §7.15.

Present subjunctive formation:

The present subjunctive is regularly formed by dropping
the *-ant* ending of the present participle of the verb you are
using and adding the endings *-e, -es, -e; -ions, -iez, -ent*.

For the present subjunctive of *avoir* and *être*, see §7.19.
See also Subjunctive, §7.15.

---

§7.8–7 Imperfect Subjunctive Tense

The *imperfect subjunctive* is used in the same ways as the
present subjunctive, that is, after certain verbs, conjunctions,
and impersonal expressions. The main difference between
these two is the time of the action. If present, use the present
subjunctive. If the action is related to the past, the imperfect
subjunctive is used, provided that the action was not completed.

Je voulais qu'il vînt. / I wanted him to come. (action not
completed; he did not come while I wanted him to come)

| Tip |

Note: The subjunctive of *venir* is used because *vouloir* requires the subjunctive *after* it. In conversational
French and informal writing, the imperfect subjunctive
is avoided. Use, instead, the present subjunctive:

Je voulais qu'il vienne. / I wanted him to come.

Imperfect subjunctive formation:

There is a shortcut to finding the forms of this difficult tense. Go straight to the 3rd person, singular, **passé simple** tense of the verb you have in mind. If the ending is **-a**, as in **parla (parler)**, drop **-a** and add **-asse, -asses, -ât**; **-assions, -assiez, -assent**. If the ending is **-it**, as in **finit (finir)** or **vendit (vendre)**, drop **-it** and add **-isse, isses, -ît; -issions, issiez, issent**.

Je le lui expliquais pour qu'elle le comprît. / I was explaining it to her so that she might understand it. (The action was not completed; the understanding was not completed at the time of the explaining.)

Tip	Note: The subjunctive of *comprendre* is used in this example because the conjunction *pour que* requires the subjunctive *after* it. Again, avoid using the imperfect subjunctive in conversation and informal writing. Use, instead, the present subjunctive: *Je le lui expliquais pour qu'elle le comprenne.*

If you find the ending **-ut**, as in many irregular -re verbs **(lire/lut)**, drop **-ut** and add **-usse, -usses, -ût; -ussions, -ussiez, -ussent**. Note the circumflex accent mark (ˆ) on **-ât, -ît, -ût**.

For the imperfect subjunctive of *avoir* and *être*, see §7.19. See also §7.15, Subjunctive.

§7.8–8 Past Indefinite Tense (Passé Composé)

This past tense is used in conversational French, correspondence, and other informal writing. The past indefinite is used more and more in literature these days and is taking the place of the past definite. It is a compound tense because it is formed with the present indicative of *avoir* or *être* (depending on which of these two auxiliaries is required to form a compound tense) plus the past participle. See §7.3 for the distinction made between verbs conjugated with *avoir* or *être*. This is the *passé composé*.

> *Il est allé à l'école.* / He went to school; He did go to school; He has gone to school.
>
> *J'ai mangé dans ce restaurant de nombreuses fois.* / I have eaten in this restaurant many times.
>
> *J'ai parlé au garçon.* / I spoke to the boy; I have spoken to the boy; I did speak to the boy.

§7.8–9 Pluperfect Tense

In French and English this tense (also called the *past perfect*) is used to express an action that happened in the past before another past action. Since it is used in relation to another past action, the other past action is expressed in either the past indefinite or the imperfect indicative in French. The pluperfect is used in formal writing and literature as well as in conversational French and informal writing. It is a compound tense because it is formed with the imperfect indicative of *avoir* or *être* (depending on which of these two auxiliaries is required to form a compound tense) plus the past participle. See §7.3 for the distinction made between verbs conjugated with *avoir* or *être.*

> *Je me suis rappelé que j'avais oublié de le lui dire.* / I remembered that I had forgotten to tell him.

| Tip | Note: It would be incorrect to say: I remembered that I forgot to tell him. The point here is that first I forgot; then I remembered. Both actions are in the past. The action that occurred in the past *before* the other past action is in the pluperfect. And in this example it is "I had forgotten" *(j'avais oublié).* |

> *J'avais étudié la leçon que le professeur a expliquée.* / I had studied the lesson that the teacher explained.

> **Tip**
>
> Note: First I studied the lesson; then the teacher explained it. Both actions are in the past. The action that occurred in the past before the other past action is in the pluperfect. And in this example it is "I had studied" *(j'avais étudié).*

J'étais fatigué ce matin parce que je n'avais pas dormi. / I was tired this morning because I had not slept.

Advanced Level

§7.8–10 Past Anterior Tense

This tense is similar to the pluperfect indicative. The main difference is that in French it is a literary tense; that is, it is used in formal writing such as history and literature. More and more French writers today use the pluperfect indicative instead of the past anterior. The past anterior is a compound tense and is formed with the *passé simple* of *avoir* or *être* (depending on which of these two auxiliaries is required to form a compound tense) plus the past participle. It is ordinarily introduced by conjunctions of time: *après que, aussitôt que, dès que, lorsque, quand.*

Quand il eut tout mangé, il partit. / When he had eaten everything, he left.

Note that most modern writers would say:

Quand il avait tout mangé, il est parti. / When he had eaten everything, he left.

§7.8–11 Future Perfect Tense

In French and English this tense (also called the *future anterior*) is used to express an action that will happen in the future *before* another future action. Since it is used in relation to another future action, the other future action is expressed in the simple future in French. It is used in conversation and informal writing as well as in formal writing and in literature. It is a compound tense because it is formed with the future of *avoir* or *être* (depending on which of these two auxiliaries is required to form a compound tense) plus the past participle of the verb you are using. In English, it is formed by using "will have" plus the past participle of the verb you are using.

Elle arrivera demain et j'aurai fini le travail. / She will arrive tomorrow and I will have finished the work.

| Tip | Note: First I will finish the work; then she will arrive. The action that will occur in the future *before* the other future action is in the future anterior. |

Quand elle arrivera demain, j'aurai fini le travail. / When she arrives tomorrow, I will have finished the work.

| Tip | Note: The idea of future time here is the same as in the preceding example. In English, the present tense is used ("When she arrives . . .") to express a near future. In French, the future is used *(Quand elle arrivera . . .)* because *quand* precedes and the action will take place in the future. |

§7.8–12 Conditional Perfect Tense

This is used in French and English to express an action that you would have done if something else had been possible; that is, you would have done something on condition that something else had been possible. It is a compound tense because it is formed with the conditional of *avoir* or *être* plus the past participle of the verb you are using. In English, it is formed by using "would have" plus the past participle.

J'aurais fait le travail si j'avais étudié. / I would have done the work if I had studied.

J'aurais fait le travail si j'en avais eu le temps. / I would have done the work if I had had the time.

§7

§7.8–13 Past Subjunctive Tense

This tense is used to express an action that took place in the past in relation to the present. It is like the past indefinite, *(passé composé)* except that the auxiliary verb *(avoir* or *être)* is in the present subjunctive. The subjunctive is used because what precedes is a certain verb, conjunction, or impersonal expression. The past subjunctive is also used in relation to a future time when another action will be completed. In French this tense is used in formal writing and in literature as well as in conversation and informal writing. It is a compound tense because it is formed with the present subjunctive of *avoir* or *être* as the auxiliary plus the past participle of the verb you are using.

An action in relation to the present:
Il est possible qu'elle soit partie. / It is possible that she has left.
Je doute qu'il ait fait cela. / I doubt that he did that.

An action that will take place in the future:
Je désire que vous soyez rentré avant dix heures. / I want you to be back before ten o'clock.

§7.8–14 Pluperfect Subjunctive Tense

This tense (also called the *past perfect*) is used for the same reasons as the imperfect subjunctive—that is, after certain verbs, conjunctions, and impersonal expressions. The main difference between the imperfect and the pluperfect subjunctive is the time of the action in the past. If the action was not completed, the imperfect subjunctive is used; if the action was completed, the pluperfect is used. In French, it is used only in formal writing and literature.

Il était possible qu'elle fût partie. / It was possible that she might have left.

Tip   Note: Avoid this tense in French because it is rarely used in conversation and informal writing. You must just be aware of it when you see it in your French readings. Use the past subjunctive instead: *Il était possible qu'elle soit partie.* See §7.8–13.

§7.8–15 Imperative Mood

The *imperative* mood is used in French and English to express a command or request. It is also used to express an indirect request made in the third person. In both languages it is formed by dropping the subject and using the present tense. There are a few exceptions in both languages when the present subjunctive is used.

> *Sortez!* / Get out! *Asseyez-vous!* / Sit down!
> *Entrez!* / Come in! *Levez-vous!* / Get up!
> *Soyez à l'heure!* / Be on time! (subjunctive used)
> *Dieu le veuille!* / May God grant it! (subjunctive used)
> *Ainsi soit-il!* / So be it! (subjunctive used)

You must drop the final *s* in the second person singular of an *-er* verb. This is done in the affirmative and negative, as in: *Mange!* / Eat! *Ne mange pas!* / Don't eat! However, when the pronouns *y* and *en* are linked to it, the *s* is retained in all regular *-er* verbs and in the verb *aller*. The reason for this is that it makes it easier to link the two elements by pronouncing the *s* as a *z*.

> *Donnes-en!* / Give some!
> *Manges-en!* / Eat some!
> *Allons!* / Let's go! (Remember that you do not drop the *s* in *nous allons*.)
> *Allons-y!* / Let's go there!
> *Va!* / Go! (Don't forget to drop the *s* in *tu vas*.)
> *Vas-y!* / Go there!

Intermediate and Advanced Levels

§7.9 PASSIVE VOICE

When verbs are used in the active voice, which is almost all the time, the subject performs the action. When the *passive* voice is used, the subject of the sentence is not the performer; the action falls on the subject. The agent (the performer) is sometimes expressed, sometimes not, as is done in English. The passive voice, therefore, is composed of the verb in the passive, which is any tense of *être* + the past participle of the verb you are using to indicate the action performed upon the subject. Since *être* is the verb used in the passive voice, the past participle of your other verb must agree with the subject in gender and number.

> *Jacqueline a été reçue à l'université.* / Jacqueline has been accepted at the university.
>
> *Ce livre est écrit par un auteur célèbre.* / This book is written by a famous author.
>
> *Cette composition a été écrite par un jeune élève.* / This composition was written by a young student.

There are certain rules you must remember about the passive voice:

- Usually the preposition *de* is used instead of *par* with such verbs as *aimer, admirer, accompagner, apprécier, voir*.
  > *Jacqueline est aimée de tout le monde.* / Jacqueline is liked (loved) by everyone.

BUT

  > *Nous avons été suivis par un chien perdu.* / We were followed by a lost dog.

- Avoid the passive voice if the thought can be expressed in the active voice with the indefinite pronoun *on* as the subject.
  > *On vend de bonnes choses dans ce magasin.* / Good things are sold in this store.
  >
  > *On parle français ici.* / French is spoken here.

- You must avoid using the passive voice with a reflexive verb. Always use a reflexive verb with an active subject.

    Elle s'appelle Jeanne. / She is called Joan.

    Comment se prononce ce mot? / How is this word pronounced?

Sometimes the passive voice is expressed in French with a reflexive verb in the active voice.

Note this example of a reflexive verb with a passive meaning:

    La bibliothèque se situe en face de l'église. / The library is located (situated) opposite the church.

§7.10 *SI* CLAUSE: A SUMMARY

When the Verb in the Si clause is in the:	The Verb in the Main or Result Clause is:
(a) present indicative	present indicative, future, or imperative
(b) imperfect indicative	conditional
(c) pluperfect indicative	conditional perfect

See **a**, **b**, and **c** below for examples.

- By *si* we mean "if." Sometimes *si* can mean "whether" and in that case, this summary does not apply because there are no restrictions about the tenses. The sequence of tenses with a *si-* clause is the same in English with an "if" clause.
    (a) *Si elle arrive, je pars.* / If she arrives, I'm leaving.
        Si elle arrive, je partirai. / If she arrives, I will leave.
        Si elle arrive, partez! / If she arrives, leave!
    (b) *Si Paul étudiait, il aurait de meilleures notes.* / If Paul studied, he would have better grades.
    (c) *Si Georges avait étudié, il aurait eu de bonnes notes.* / If George had studied, he would have had good grades.
- Review §7.8–5, Conditional Present Tense, on page 93.

§7

§7.11 SPECIAL USES OF COMMON VERBS

CONNAÎTRE / TO KNOW; TO BE ACQUAINTED WITH; TO MAKE THE ACQUAINTANCE OF

- Present
  Connaissez-vous Mme Vallois? / Do you know Mrs. Vallois?
  Non, je ne la connais pas. / No, I don't know her.
- Conditional
  Mon oncle connaissait New York comme sa poche. / My uncle
    knew New York like the back of his hand.
- Passé composé
  In the passé composé, *connaître* can mean "to meet" or "to make
    the acquaintance of."
  Mon père a connu ma mère au Luxembourg. / My father met my
    mother in Luxembourg.
  See *Savoir* and *Connaître*, page 107.

DEVOIR / TO OWE; OUGHT TO

- Present
  Je dois étudier. / I have to study; I must study; I am supposed to
    study.
  Elle doit être fatiguée après le marathon. / She must be tired after
    the marathon. or She's probably tired after the marathon.
  Mon père doit avoir cinquante ans. / My father must be 50 years
    old.
- Imperfect
  Je devais étudier. / I had to study; I was supposed to study.
  Quand j'étais à l'école, je devais toujours étudier. / When I was in
    school, I always had to study.
  Ma mère devait avoir cinquante ans quand elle est morte. / My
    mother was probably 50 years old when she died.
- Future
  Je devrai étudier. / I will have to study.
  Nous devrons faire le travail ce soir. / We will have to do the work
    this evening.

• Conditional

Je devrais étudier. / I ought to study; I should study.

Vous devriez étudier davantage. / You ought to study more; You should study more.

• Past indefinite

Je ne suis pas allé(e) au cinéma parce que j'ai dû étudier. / I did not go to the movies because I had to study.

J'ai dû prendre l'autobus parce qu'il n'y avait pas de train à cette heure-là. / I had to take the bus because there was no train at that hour.

Robert n'est pas ici. / Robert is not here.

Il a dû partir. / He must have left; He has probably left; He had to leave.

• Conditional perfect

J'aurais dû étudier! / I should have studied!

Vous auriez dû me dire la vérité. / You should have told me the truth.

• With a direct or an indirect object there is still another meaning.

Je dois de l'argent. / I owe some money.

Je le lui dois. / I owe it to him (to her).

POUVOIR / TO BE ABLE TO, CAN

§7

• Present

Je ne peux pas sortir aujourd'hui parce que je suis malade. / I cannot (am unable to) go out today because I am sick.

Est-ce que je peux entrer? Puis-je entrer? / May I come in?

Madame Marin peut être malade. / Mrs. Marin may be sick.

This use of *pouvoir* suggests possibility.

Je n'en peux plus. / I can't go on any longer.
This use suggests physical exhaustion.

Il se peut. / It is possible.
This use as a reflexive verb suggests possibility.

> *Cela ne se peut pas.* / That can't be done.
> This use as a reflexive verb suggests impossibility.

- Conditional
    Pourriez-vous me prêter dix euros?/ Could you lend me ten euros?

- Conditional perfect
    Auriez-vous pu venir chez moi? / Could you have come to my place?
    Ils auraient pu rater le train. / They might have missed the train.

VOULOIR / TO WANT

- Present
    Je veux aller en France. / I want to go to France.
    Je veux bien sortir avec vous ce soir. / I am willing to go out with you this evening.
    Voulez-vous bien vous asseoir? / Would you be good enough to sit down?
    Que veut dire ce mot? / What does this word mean?
    Que voulez-vous dire? / What do you mean?
    Qu'est-ce que cela veut dire? / What does that mean?

- Conditional
    Je voudrais un café crème, s'il vous plaît. / I would like coffee with cream, please.

- Imperative
    Veuillez vous asseoir. / Kindly sit down.
    Veuillez accepter mes meilleurs sentiments. / Please accept my best regards.

SAVOIR / TO KNOW (a fact)

- Present
    Je sais la réponse. / I know the answer.
    Je sais lire en français. / I know how to read in French.

- Conditional

  Sauriez-vous où est le docteur? / Would you know where the doctor is?

  Je ne saurais penser à tout! / I can't think of everything!

- Imperative

  Sachons-le bien! / Let's be well aware of it!

  Sachez que votre père vient de mourir. / Be informed that your father has just died.

- Passé composé

  In the passé composé, *savoir* means "to find out."

  J'ai su que le tableau valait mille dollars. / I found out that the painting was worth a thousand dollars.

SAVOIR AND CONNAÎTRE

The main difference between the meaning of these two verbs in the sense of "to know" is that *connaître* means merely to be acquainted with; for example, to be acquainted with a person, a city, a neighborhood, a country, the title of a book, the works of an author.

Savez-vous la réponse? / Do you know the answer?

Savez-vous quelle heure il est? / Do you know what time it is?

Connaissez-vous cette dame? / Do you know this lady?

Connaissez-vous Paris? / Do you know Paris?

Connaissez-vous ce livre? Do you know this book?

ENTENDRE AND COMPRENDRE

The main difference between the meaning of these two verbs is that *entendre* means "to hear" and *comprendre* "to understand." Sometimes *entendre* can mean "to understand" or "to mean."

Entendez-vous la musique? / Do you hear the music?

Comprenez-vous la leçon? / Do you understand the lesson?

"M'entends-tu?!" dit la mère à l'enfant. "Ne fais pas cela!" / "Do you understand me?!" says the mother to the child. "Don't do that!"

§7

*Je ne comprends pas M. Grossier parce qu'il parle la bouche
  pleine.* / I do not understand Mr. Grossier because he is talking
  with his mouth full.

Qu'entendez-vous par là? / What do you mean by that? What are
  you insinuating by that remark?

*Je vous entends, mais je ne vous comprends pas; expliquez-vous,
  s'il vous plaît.* / I hear you, but I don't understand you; explain
  yourself, please.

QUITTER, PARTIR, SORTIR, **AND** LAISSER

These four verbs all mean "to leave," but note the differences
in their uses:

• Use *quitter* when you state a direct object noun or pronoun
  that could be a person or a place.

  J'ai quitté mes amis devant le théâtre. / I left my friends in front of
    the theater.

  J'ai quitté la maison à six heures du matin. / I left the house at six
    in the morning.

• Use *partir* when there is no direct object noun or pronoun.

  Elle est partie tout de suite. / She left immediately.

However, if you use the preposition *de* after *partir*, you
may add a direct object, but it would be the object of the
preposition *de*, not of the verb *partir*.

  Elle est partie de la maison à six heures du matin. / She left (from)
    the house at six in the morning.

• Use *sortir*, in the sense of "to go out." With no direct
  object:

  Elle est sortie il y a une heure. / She went out an hour ago.

However, if you use the preposition *de* after *sortir*, you may
add a direct object, but it would be object of the preposition
de, not of the verb *sortir*.

  Elle est sortie de la maison il y a une heure. / She left (went out of)
    the house an hour ago.

> **Tip**
>
> Note that *sortir* can also be conjugated with *avoir* to form a compound tense, but then the meaning changes because it can take a direct object.
>
> *Elle a sorti son mouchoir pour se moucher.* / She took out her handkerchief to wipe her nose.
>
> *Elle a sorti son mouchoir pour moucher son enfant.* / She took out her handkerchief to wipe her child's nose.

- Use *laisser* when you leave behind something that is not stationary; in other words, something movable, for example, books and articles of clothing.

  J'ai laissé mes livres sur la table dans la cuisine. / I left my books on the table in the kitchen.

  J'ai laissé mon imperméable à la maison. / I left my raincoat at home.

Note that *laisser* also has the meaning "to let, allow a person to do something":

  J'ai laissé mon ami partir. / I let (allowed) my friend to leave.

> **Tip**
>
> *Partir* / to leave, go away contains an *a* and so does "away."
>
> *Sortir* / to go out contains an *o* and so does "out."

FALLOIR

- *Falloir* is an impersonal verb, which means that it is used only in the third person singular (*il* form) in all the tenses; its primary meaning is "to be necessary." Also, "you have to."

  Il faut étudier pour avoir de bonnes notes. / You have to study in order to have good grades.

  Faut-il le faire tout de suite? / Is it necessary to do it at once?

  Oui, il le faut. / Yes, it is (understood: necessary to do it).

The use of the neuter direct object *le* is needed to show emphasis and to complete the thought.

  Il faut être honnête. / It is necessary to be honest.

In the negative:

Il ne faut pas être malhonnête. / One must not be dishonest.

Note that *il faut* in the negative means "one must not."
Il ne faut pas fumer. / One must not smoke.

Proverbe français: *Il ne faut pas condamner sans entendre.* / One must not condemn without a hearing. (No one should be condemned unheard.)

---

§7.12 OTHER VERBS WITH SPECIAL MEANINGS

apprendre à quelqu'un à + infinitive / to teach somebody + inf. *Mon père m'a appris à pêcher.* / My father taught me to fish.

arriver / to happen *Qu'est-ce qui est arrivé?* / What happened?

avoir / to have something the matter *Qu'est-ce que vous avez?* / What's the matter with you?

entendre dire que / to hear it said that, hear that *J'entends dire que Robert s'est marié.* / I hear that Robert got married.

entendre parler de / to hear of, about *J'ai entendu parler d'un grand changement dans l'administration.* / I've heard about a big change in the administration.

envoyer chercher / to send for *Je vais envoyer chercher le médecin.* / I'm going to send for the doctor.

être à quelqu'un / to belong to someone *Ce livre est à moi.* / This book belongs to me.

faillir + infinitive to almost do something *Le bébé a failli tomber.* / The baby almost fell.

mettre / to put on *Gisèle a mis sa plus jolie robe.* / Gisèle put on her prettiest dress.

mettre la table / to set the table

profiter de / to take advantage of

rendre visite à / to pay a visit to *J'ai rendu visite à mon cousin en Floride.* / I paid a visit to (visited) my cousin in Florida.
Note: Use *visiter* when you visit a place: *Nous avons visité le Musée de la civilisation à Québec.* / We visited the Museum of Civilization in Quebec City.

venir à / to happen to *Si nous venons à nous rencontrer, nous pourrons prendre une tasse de café.* / If we happen to meet each other, we can have a cup of coffee.

venir de + infinitive / to have just done something *Joseph vient de partir.* / Joseph has just left; *Barbara venait de partir quand Françoise est arrivée.* / Barbara had just left when Françoise arrived.

§7.13 INFINITIVES

• In English, an *infinitive* contains the preposition "to" in front of it: "to give," "to finish," "to sell." In French an infinitive has a certain ending. There are three major types of infinitives in French: those that end in *-er* (*donner*); those that end in *-ir* (*finir*); and those that end in *-re* (*vendre*).

> **Tip** Verbs that end in *-oir* are considered to be a separate type of *-ir* verb. They do not follow the same pattern and must be learned individually. Some examples: *devoir* (to have to, to owe), *recevoir* (to receive), *savoir* (to know), *vouloir* (to want).

• Make an infinitive negative in French by placing *ne pas* in front of it.
   Je vous dis de ne pas sortir. / I am telling you not to go out.

• The infinitive is often used after a verb of perception to express an action that is in progress.
   J'entends quelqu'un chanter. / I hear somebody singing.
   Je vois venir les enfants. / I see the children coming.

   Some common verbs of perception are: *apercevoir* / to perceive, *écouter* / to listen to, *entendre* / to hear, *regarder* / to look at, *sentir* / to feel, *voir* / to see.

• There are certain French verbs that take either the preposition *à* or *de* + infinitive.
   Il commence à pleuvoir. / It is beginning to rain.
   Il a cessé de pleuvoir. / It has stopped raining.

- *Avant de* and *sans* + infinitive

  Sylvie a mangé avant de sortir. / Sylvia ate before going out.

  André est parti sans dire un mot. / Andrew left without saying a word.

Note also the prepositions *afin de* and *pour*.

  Marie est allée en France afin d'améliorer son français. / Mary went to France (in order) to improve her French.

  J'ai mis mon manteau pour sortir. / I put on my coat to go out.

- Use of infinitive instead of a verb form

  Generally speaking, an infinitive is used instead of a verb form if the subject in a sentence is the same for the actions expressed.

  Je veux faire le travail. / I want to do the work.

> **Tip** But, if there are two different subjects, you must use a new clause and a new verb form. (Note that the wishes expressed in the following two statements require the subjunctive mood.)

  Je veux que vous fassiez le travail. / I want you to do the work.

  Je préfère que vous vous couchiez tôt. / I prefer that you go to bed early.

BUT

  Préférer does not require the subjunctive when you are not using the expression *préférer que*.

  Je préfère me coucher tôt. / I prefer to go to bed early.

- Past infinitive

  In French the past infinitive is expressed by using the infinitive form of *avoir* or *être* + the past participle of the main verb being used.

  Après avoir quitté la maison, Monsieur et Madame Dubé sont allés au cinéma. / After leaving (having left) the house, Mr. and Mrs. Dubé went to the movies.

  Après être arrivée, Jeanne a envoyé un texto à sa mère. / After arriving (having arrived), Jeanne texted her mother.

§7.14 CAUSATIVE (CAUSAL) *FAIRE*

The construction *faire* + infinitive means to have something done by someone. The causative *faire* can be in any tense, but it must be followed by an infinitive.

Examples with nouns and pronouns as direct and indirect objects:

> *Madame Smith fait travailler ses élèves dans la classe de français.* /
> Mrs. Smith makes her students work in French class.
>
> In this example, the direct object is the noun *élèves* and it is placed right after the infinitive.

> *Madame Smith les fait travailler dans la classe de français.* /
> Mrs. Smith makes them work (has them work) in French class.
>
> In this example, the direct object is the pronoun *les*, referring to *les élèves*. It is placed in front of the verb form of *faire*, where it logically belongs.

> *Madame Smith fait lire la phrase.* / Mrs. Smith is having the sentence read. or Mrs. Smith has the sentence read.
>
> In this example, the direct object is the noun *phrase* and it is placed right after the infinitive, as in the first example.

> *Madame Smith la fait lire.* / Mrs. Smith is having it read.
>
> In this example, the direct object is the pronoun *la*, referring to *la phrase*. It is placed in front of the verb form of *faire*, where it logically belongs. This is like the second example, but here the direct object is a thing. In the other two examples, the direct object is a person.

§7.15 SUBJUNCTIVE

The subjunctive is not a tense, but a *mood*, or mode. Usually when we speak in French or English, we use the indicative mood, but the subjunctive mood in French must be used in specific cases. The subjunctive is used:

After Certain Conjunctions

When the following conjunctions introduce a new clause, the verb in that new clause is usually in the subjunctive mood.

à condition que / on condition that
à moins que / unless
afin que / in order that, so that
au cas où / in case
bien que / although
de crainte que / for fear that
de manière que / so that
de peur que / for fear that
de sorte que / so that
en attendant que / until
jusqu'à ce que / until
malgré que / although
pour que / in order that
pourvu que / provided that
quoique / although

Je vous explique pour que vous compreniez. / I am explaining to you so that you will understand.

Bien que vous soyez malade, vous devez assister à la réunion. / Although you are ill, you must attend the meeting.

Au cas où nous soyons d'accord . . . / In case we are in agreement . . .

After Indefinite Expressions

> *où que* / wherever
> *quel que* / whatever
> *qui que* / whoever
> *quoi que* / whatever, no matter what

After an Indefinite Antecedent

The subjunctive is needed after an indefinite antecedent because the person or thing desired may possibly not exist; or, if it does exist, you may never find it.

> *Je cherche une personne qui soit honnête.* / I am looking for a person who is honest.
>
> *Je cherche un appartement qui ne soit pas trop cher.* / I am looking for an apartment that is not too expensive.
>
> *Connaissez-vous quelqu'un qui puisse réparer mon ordinateur une fois pour toutes?* / Do you know someone who can repair my computer once and for all?
>
> *Y a-t-il un élève qui comprenne le subjonctif?* / Is there a student who understands the subjunctive?

After a Superlative Expressing an Opinion

Tip
The most common superlatives expressing an opinion are: *le seul (la seule)* / the only, *le premier (la première)* / the first, *le dernier (la dernière)* / the last, *le plus petit (la plus petite)* / the smallest, *le plus grand (la plus grande)* / the biggest, *le meilleur (la meilleure)* / the best.

> *A mon avis, Marie est la seule étudiante qui comprenne le subjonctif.* / In my opinion, Mary is the only student who understands the subjunctive.
>
> *Selon l'entraîneur, Martine est la meilleure footballeuse qu'il ait jamais vue.* / According to the coach, Martine is the best soccer player he has ever seen.

§7

After *que*, Meaning "Let" or "May"

The subjunctive is required after *que* to express a wish, an order, or a command in the third person singular or plural.

Qu'il parte! / Let him leave!

Que Dieu nous pardonne! / May God forgive us!

Qu'ils s'en aillent! / Let them go away!

After Certain Impersonal Expressions

c'est dommage que / it's a pity that
il est bizarre que / it is odd that
il est bon que / it is good that
il est douteux que / it is doubtful that
il est essentiel que / it is essential that
il est étonnant que / it is astonishing that
il est étrange que / it is strange that
il est heureux que / it is fortunate that
il est honteux que / it is a shame that
il est important que / it is important that
il est impossible que / it is impossible that
il est nécessaire que / it is necessary that
il est possible que / it is possible that
il est regrettable que / it is regrettable that
il est temps que / it is time that
il est urgent que / it is urgent that
il faut que / it is necessary that
il se peut que / it may be that
il semble que / it seems that
il vaut mieux que / it is better that

Examples:

Il est important que vous arriviez à l'heure. / It is important that you arrive on time.

Il est urgent que je prenne rendez-vous avec M. Dupin. / It is urgent that I make an appointment with Mr. Dupin.

After Certain Verbs Expressing Doubt, Emotion, or Wishing

aimer que / to like that
aimer mieux que / to prefer that
attendre que / to wait until
s'attendre à ce que / to expect that
avoir peur que / to be afraid that
craindre que / to fear that
défendre que / to forbid that
désirer que / to desire that
douter que / to doubt that
empêcher que / to prevent that
s'étonner que / to be astonished that
être bien aise que / to be pleased that
être content que / to be glad that
être désolé que / to be distressed that, sorry that
être étonné que / to be astonished that
être heureux que / to be happy that
être joyeux que / to be joyful that
être ravi que / to be delighted that
être triste que / to be sad that
exiger que / to demand that
se fâcher que / to be angry that
insister que / to insist that
ordonner que / to order that
préférer que / to prefer that
regretter que / to regret that
souhaiter que / to wish that
tenir à ce que / to insist upon
vouloir que / to want

Examples:

J'aimerais que vous restiez ici. / I would like you to stay here.

J'aime mieux que vous restiez ici. / I prefer that you stay here.

Nous nous attendons à ce qu'elle vienne immédiatement. / We expect her to come immediately.

Ta mère est contente que tu sois heureux. / Your mother is glad that you are happy.

Attendez que je finisse mon dîner. / Wait until I finish my dinner.

After Verbs of Believing and Thinking

Such verbs are *croire*, *penser*, *trouver* (meaning "to think, to have an impression"), and *espérer* when used in the negative or interrogative.

Je ne pense pas qu'il soit coupable. / I don't think that he is guilty.

Croyez-vous qu'il dise la vérité? / Do you believe he is telling the truth?

Trouvez-vous qu'il y ait beaucoup de crimes dans la société d'aujourd'hui? / Do you find (think) that there are many crimes in today's society?

§7.16 SUMMARY OF TENSES AND MOODS

The 7 simple tenses	The 7 compound tenses
Present indicative	Past indefinite (*passé composé*)
Imperfect indicative	Pluperfect indicative
Past definite (Simple past)	Past anterior
Future	Future perfect
Conditional	Conditional perfect
Present subjunctive	Past subjunctive
Imperfect subjunctive	Pluperfect subjunctive
Imperative or Command	

§7.17 SPELLING IRREGULARITIES OF SOME COMMON VERBS (ORTHOGRAPHICAL CHANGES)

The verbs conjugated here all undergo certain spelling changes in the tenses indicated.*

In French, you must include a subject or subject pronoun when you conjugate a verb (for example, *je mange*, *tu parles*). However, in the following tables, the subject pronouns have been omitted in order to eliminate repetition and to emphasize the verb forms. The subject pronouns are:

	Singular	Plural
1st	*je (j')*	*nous*
2nd	*tu*	*vous*
3rd	*il, elle, on*	*ils, elles*

§7

*Review §1., Guide to Pronouncing French Sounds, pages 1–4, to understand why some verb forms change in spelling.

PRESENT INDICATIVE

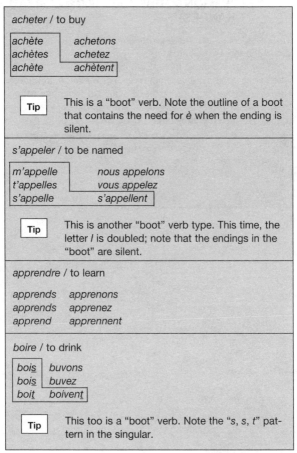

acheter / to buy

achète	achetons
achètes	achetez
achète	achètent

Tip This is a "boot" verb. Note the outline of a boot that contains the need for *è* when the ending is silent.

s'appeler / to be named

m'appelle	nous appelons
t'appelles	vous appelez
s'appelle	s'appellent

Tip This is another "boot" verb type. This time, the letter *l* is doubled; note that the endings in the "boot" are silent.

apprendre / to learn

apprends	apprenons
apprends	apprenez
apprend	apprennent

boire / to drink

bois	buvons
bois	buvez
boit	boivent

Tip This too is a "boot" verb. Note the "*s, s, t*" pattern in the singular.

commencer / to begin, start

commence	*commençons*
commences	*commencez*
commence	*commencent*

comprendre / to understand (like *prendre,* page 125; add com- at the beginning of *prendre*)

conduire / to drive; to lead

conduis	*conduisons*
conduis	*conduisez*
conduit	*conduisent*

connaître / to know, to be acquainted with

connais	*connaissons*
connais	*connaissez*
connaît	*connaissent*

courir / to run

cours	*courons*
cours	*courez*
court	*courent*

croire / to believe

crois	*croyons*
crois	*croyez*
croit	*croient*

devenir / to become

deviens	*devenons*
deviens	*devenez*
devient	*deviennent*

§7

devoir / to owe; to have to

dois	devons
dois	devez
doit	doivent

dire / to say; to tell

dis	disons
dis	dites
dit	disent

dormir / to sleep

dors	dormons
dors	dormez
dort	dorment

écrire / to write

écris	écrivons
écris	écrivez
écrit	écrivent

envoyer / to send

envoie	envoyons
envoies	envoyez
envoie	envoient

Tip	You must change *y* to *i* before a mute *e* when you conjugate a verb that ends in *-oyer*.

espérer / to hope

espère	espérons
espères	espérez
espère	espèrent

falloir / to be necessary

il faut

---

se lever / to get up

me lève	nous levons
te lèves	vous levez
se lève	se lèvent

> **Tip** The *e* changes to *è* before a syllable with a mute *e*.

---

lire / to read

lis	lisons
lis	lisez
lit	lisent

---

manger / to eat

mange	mangeons
manges	mangez
mange	mangent

> **Tip** The *e* in *mangeons* keeps the soft *g* sound before the letter *o*.

---

mettre / to place, put; to put on

mets	mettons
mets	mettez
met	mettent

---

mourir / to die

meurs	mourons
meurs	mourez
meurt	meurent

§7

nager / to swim

nage	nageons
nages	nagez
nage	nagent

> **Tip** The *e* in *nageons* keeps the soft *g* sound before the letter *o*.

naître / to be born

nais	naissons
nais	naissez
naît	naissent

offrir / to offer

offre	offrons
offres	offrez
offre	offrent

ouvrir / to open

ouvre	ouvrons
ouvres	ouvrez
ouvre	ouvrent

partir / to leave

pars	partons
pars	partez
part	partent

pleuvoir / to rain
il pleut

pouvoir / to be able, can		Note: In the affirmative, it is most common to say "Je peux." In the inverted interrogative, you should say "Puis-je?"
peu<u>x</u> OR pui<u>s</u>	pouvons	
peu<u>x</u>	pouvez	
peu<u>t</u>	peuven<u>t</u>	

---

préférer / to prefer

préfère	préférons
préfères	préférez
préfère	préfèrent

Tip	The é changes to è before a syllable with a mute e.

---

prendre / to take

prends	prenons
prends	prenez
prend	prennent

---

protéger / to protect

protège	protégeons
protèges	protégez
protège	protègent

Tip	There are two spelling changes in *protéger*. An e is added in the *nous* form to keep the soft *g* sound; the é changes to è before a syllable with a mute e.

---

recevoir / to receive

reçoi<u>s</u>	recevons
reçoi<u>s</u>	recevez
reçoi<u>t</u>	reçoivent

§7

revenir / to return, come back (like *venir,* below; add *re-* at the beginning of *venir*)

rire / to laugh

ris	rions
ris	riez
rit	rient

savoir / to know (a fact)

sais	savons
sais	savez
sait	savent

servir / to serve

sers	servons
sers	servez
sert	servent

sortir / to go out; to leave

sors	sortons
sors	sortez
sort	sortent

tenir / to hold

tiens	tenons
tiens	tenez
tient	tiennent

venir / to come

viens	venons
viens	venez
vient	viennent

vivre / to live

vis	vivons
vis	vivez
vit	vivent

voir / to see

vois	voyons
vois	voyez
voit	voient

vouloir / to want

veux	voulons
veux	voulez
veut	veulent

voyager / to travel

voyage	voyageons
voyages	voyagez
voyage	voyagent

| Tip | The *e* in *voyageons* keeps the soft *g* sound before the letter *o*. |

§7

IMPERFECT INDICATIVE

To form the imperfect tense, go to the present tense *nous* form of the verb, drop *-ons*, and add *ais, ais, ait, ions, iez,* or *aient.* (See §7.8–2.)

---

apprendre / to learn

apprenais	apprenions
apprenais	appreniez
apprenait	apprenaient

---

boire / to drink

buvais	buvions
buvais	buviez
buvait	buvaient

---

commencer / to begin, to start

commençais	commencions
commençais	commenciez
commençait	commençaient

Tip   Remember that you need a *ç* before the letter *a* in the imperfect tense to keep the *s* sound.

---

comprendre / to understand (like *prendre,* page 131; add *com-* at the beginning of *prendre*)

---

conduire / to drive; to lead

conduisais	conduisions
conduisais	conduisiez
conduisait	conduisaient

---

connaître / to know, be acquainted with

connaissais	connaissions
connaissais	connaissiez
connaissait	connaissaient

courir / to run

courais	courions
courais	couriez
courait	couraient

croire / to believe

croyais	croyions
croyais	croyiez
croyait	croyaient

devenir / to become

devenais	devenions
devenais	deveniez
devenait	devenaient

devoir / to owe; to have to

devais	devions
devais	deviez
devait	devaient

dire / to say; to tell

disais	disions
disais	disiez
disait	disaient

dormir / to sleep

dormais	dormions
dormais	dormiez
dormait	dormaient

écrire / to write

écrivais	écrivions
écrivais	écriviez
écrivait	écrivaient

étudier / to study
étudiais étudiions
étudiais étudiiez
étudiait étudiaient

| Tip | It is correct for the *nous* and *vous* forms of *étudier* to contain *ii* in the imperfect. Remember, if you study imperfectly, your eyes (*ii*) may hurt. |

falloir / to be necessary

il fallait

lire / to read

lisais   lisions
lisais   lisiez
lisait   lisaient

manger / to eat

mangeais | *mangions*
mangeais | *mangiez*
mangeait   *mangeaient*

| Tip | Remember to add an *e* to keep the soft *g* sound before the letter *a*. |

mourir / to die
mourais   mourions
mourais   mouriez
mourait   mouraient

nager / to swim

nageais	nagions
nageais	nagiez
nageait	nageaient

Tip Remember to add an *e* to keep the soft *g* sound before the letter *a*.

naître / to be born

naissais naissions
naissais naissiez
naissait naissaient

offrir / to offer

offrais offrions
offrais offriez
offrait offraient

ouvrir / to open

ouvrais ouvrions
ouvrais ouvriez
ouvrait ouvraient

partir / to leave

partais partions
partais partiez
partait partaient

pleuvoir / to rain
il pleuvait

prendre / to take

prenais prenions
prenais preniez
prenait prenaient

§7

protéger / to protect

protég<u>e</u>ais	protégions
protég<u>e</u>ais	protégiez
protég<u>e</u>ait	protég<u>e</u>aient

Tip — Add an *e* before the letter *a* to retain the soft *g* sound; because the ending is not silent in the imperfect, there is no need to change *é* to *è*.

revenir / to return, to come back (like *venir,* page 133; add *re-* at the beginning of *venir*)

rire / to laugh

riais	riions
riais	riiez
riait	riaient

Tip — As with the verb *étudier*, it is correct for the *nous* and *vous* forms of *rire* to contain *ii* in the imperfect.

savoir / to know (a fact)

savais	savions
savais	saviez
savait	savaient

servir / to serve

servais	servions
servais	serviez
servait	servaient

sortir / to go out; to leave

sortais	sortions
sortais	sortiez
sortait	sortaient

tenir / to hold

tenais	*tenions*
tenais	*teniez*
tenait	*tenaient*

venir / to come

venais	*venions*
venais	*veniez*
venait	*venaient*

vivre / to live

vivais	*vivions*
vivais	*viviez*
vivait	*vivaient*

voir / to see

voyais	*voyions*
voyais	*voyiez*
voyait	*voyaient*

vouloir / to want

voulais	*voulions*
voulais	*vouliez*
voulait	*voulaient*

§7

voyager / to travel

voyageais	*voyagions*
voyageais	*voyagiez*
voyageait	*voyageaient*

Tip	Remember to add an *e* to keep the soft *g* sound before the letter *a*.

§7.18 BASIC NEGATIONS OF VERBS

The common negations of verbs are *ne* + verb + any of the following:

aucun, aucune / no, not one, not any

> *Je n'ai aucun livre.* / I have no book.
>
> *Robert n'a aucune chance de gagner le match.* / Robert has no chance of winning the game.

guère / hardly, scarcely

> *Paul ne parle guère.* / Paul hardly (scarcely) talks.

jamais / never

> *Jean n'étudie jamais.* / John never studies.

ni . . . ni / neither . . . nor

> *Je n'ai ni argent ni billet.* / I have neither money nor tickets.

nul, nulle / no, not any

> *Je n'en ai nul besoin.* / I have no need of it.
>
> *Je ne vais nulle part.* / I'm not going anywhere.

pas / not

> *Je n'ai pas de papier.* / I haven't any paper. or I do not have any paper.

pas du tout / not at all

> *Je ne comprends pas du tout.* / I do not understand at all.

personne / nobody, no one, not anybody

> *Je ne vois personne.* / I don't see anybody. I see no one.

plus / any longer, no more, not anymore

> *Mon père ne travaille plus.* / My father doesn't work anymore.

point / not at all

> *Cet enfant n'a point d'argent.* / This child has no money at all.

que / only, but only

> *Je n'ai que deux euros.* / I have (but) only two euros.

rien / nothing

> *Je n'ai rien sur moi.* / I have nothing on me.

Tip

Note that all these negations require *ne* in front of the main verb. Also note that *aucun, aucune, nul, nulle, personne, rien* can be used as subjects and you still need to use *ne* in front of the verb.

Personne n'entend le bruit. / Nobody hears the noise.

Rien n'est jamais parfait. / Nothing is ever perfect.

In spoken French, you may hear someone drop the *ne*:
Ce n'est pas vrai! / It isn't true! → *C'est pas vrai!* / It isn't true!

Tip

Une devinette / a riddle

J'ai des yeux mais je n'ai pas de paupières et je vis dans l'eau. Qui suis-je? / I have eyes but I don't have eyelids and I live in the water. Who am I?

un poisson / a fish

§7.19 FOUR IRREGULAR VERBS, FULLY CONJUGATED

The following irregular verbs—*aller*, *avoir*, *être*, and *faire*—have been fully conjugated in all their tenses because they are so frequently used.

aller / to go
Present participle: *allant*   **Past participle:** *allé(e)(s)*

The Seven Simple Tenses		The Seven Compound Tenses	
Singular	**Plural**	**Singular**	**Plural**
Present indicative		Past indefinite (passé composé)	
vais	*allons*	*suis allé(e)*	*sommes allé(e)s*
vas	*allez*	*es allé(e)*	*êtes allé(e)(s)*
va	*vont*	*est allé(e)*	*sont allé(e)s*
Imperfect indicative		Pluperfect OR Past perfect indicative	
allais	*allions*	*étais allé(e)*	*étions allé(e)s*
allais	*alliez*	*étais allé(e)*	*étiez allé(e)(s)*
allait	*allaient*	*était allé(e)*	*étaient allé(e)s*
Simple past		Past anterior	
allai	*allâmes*	*fus allé(e)*	*fûmes allé(e)s*
allas	*allâtes*	*fus allé(e)*	*fûtes allé(e)(s)*
alla	*allèrent*	*fut allé(e)*	*furent allé(e)s*
Future		Future perfect OR Future anterior	
irai	*irons*	*serai allé(e)*	*serons allé(e)s*
iras	*irez*	*seras allé(e)*	*serez allé(e)(s)*
ira	*iront*	*sera allé(e)*	*seront allé(e)s*
Conditional		Conditional perfect	
irais	*irions*	*serais allé(e)*	*serions allé(e)s*
irais	*iriez*	*serais allé(e)*	*seriez allé(e)(s)*
irait	*iraient*	*serait allé(e)*	*seraient allé(e)s*
Present subjunctive		Past subjunctive	
aille	*allions*	*sois allé(e)*	*soyons allé(e)s*
ailles	*alliez*	*sois allé(e)*	*soyez allé(e)(s)*
aille	*aillent*	*soit allé(e)*	*soient allé(e)s*
Imperfect subjunctive		Pluperfect OR Past perfect subjunctive	
allasse	*allassions*	*fusse allé(e)*	*fussions allé(e)s*
allasses	*allassiez*	*fusses allé(e)*	*fussiez allé(e)(s)*
allât	*allassent*	*fût allé(e)*	*fussent allé(e)s*

Imperative OR Command

va

allons

allez

avoir / **to have**

Present participle: *ayant*   **Past participle:** *eu*

The Seven Simple Tenses		The Seven Compound Tenses	
Singular	**Plural**	**Singular**	**Plural**
Present indicative		Past indefinite (passé composé)	
ai	*avons*	*ai eu*	*avons eu*
as	*avez*	*as eu*	*avez eu*
a	*ont*	*a eu*	*ont eu*
Imperfect indicative		Pluperfect OR Past perfect indicative	
avais	*avions*	*avais eu*	*avions eu*
avais	*aviez*	*avais eu*	*aviez eu*
avait	*avaient*	*avait eu*	*avaient eu*
Simple past		Past anterior	
eus	*eûmes*	*eus eu*	*eûmes eu*
eus	*eûtes*	*eus eu*	*eûtes eu*
eut	*eurent*	*eut eu*	*eurent eu*
Future		Future perfect OR Future anterior	
aurai	*aurons*	*aurai eu*	*aurons eu*
auras	*aurez*	*auras eu*	*aurez eu*
aura	*auront*	*aura eu*	*auront eu*
Conditional		Conditional perfect	
aurais	*aurions*	*aurais eu*	*aurions eu*
aurais	*auriez*	*aurais eu*	*auriez eu*
aurait	*auraient*	*aurait eu*	*auraient eu*
Present subjunctive		Past subjunctive	
aie	*ayons*	*aie eu*	*ayons eu*
aies	*ayez*	*aies eu*	*ayez eu*
ait	*aient*	*ait eu*	*aient eu*
Imperfect subjunctive		Pluperfect OR Past perfect subjunctive	
eusse	*eussions*	*eusse eu*	*eussions eu*
eusses	*eussiez*	*eusses eu*	*eussiez eu*
eût	*eussent*	*eût eu*	*eussent eu*
Imperative OR Command			
aie			
ayons			
ayez			

§7

être / **to be**

Present participle: *étant*	**Past participle:** *été*

The Seven Simple Tenses	The Seven Compound Tenses

Singular	**Plural**	**Singular**	**Plural**
Present indicative		Past indefinite (passé composé)	
suis	*sommes*	*ai été*	*avons été*
es	*êtes*	*as été*	*avez été*
est	*sont*	*a été*	*ont été*
Imperfect indicative		Pluperfect OR Past perfect indicative	
étais	*étions*	*avais été*	*avions été*
étais	*étiez*	*avais été*	*aviez été*
était	*étaient*	*avait été*	*avaient été*
Simple past		Past anterior	
fus	*fûmes*	*eus été*	*eûmes été*
fus	*fûtes*	*eus été*	*eûtes été*
fut	*furent*	*eut été*	*eurent été*
Future		Future perfect OR Future anterior	
serai	*serons*	*aurai été*	*aurons été*
seras	*serez*	*auras été*	*aurez été*
sera	*seront*	*aura été*	*auront été*
Conditional		Conditional perfect	
serais	*serions*	*aurais été*	*aurions été*
serais	*seriez*	*aurais été*	*auriez été*
serait	*seraient*	*aurait été*	*auraient été*
Present subjunctive		Past subjunctive	
sois	*soyons*	*aie été*	*ayons été*
sois	*soyez*	*aies été*	*ayez été*
soit	*soient*	*ait été*	*aient été*
Imperfect subjunctive		Pluperfect OR Past perfect subjunctive	
fusse	*fussions*	*eusse été*	*eussions été*
fusses	*fussiez*	*eusses été*	*eussiez été*
fût	*fussent*	*eût été*	*eussent été*

Imperative OR Command

sois

soyons

soyez

faire / **to do, to make**

Present participle: *faisant* **Past participle:** *fait*

The Seven Simple Tenses		The Seven Compound Tenses	
Singular	**Plural**	**Singular**	**Plural**
Present indicative		Past indefinite (passé composé)	
fais	faisons	ai fait	avons fait
fais	faites	as fait	avez fait
fait	font	a fait	ont fait
Imperfect indicative		Pluperfect OR Past perfect indicative	
faisais	faisions	avais fait	avions fait
faisais	faisiez	avais fait	aviez fait
faisait	faisaient	avait fait	avaient fait
Simple past		Past anterior	
fis	fîmes	eus fait	eûmes fait
fis	fîtes	eus fait	eûtes fait
fit	firent	eut fait	eurent fait
Future		Future perfect OR Future anterior	
ferai	ferons	aurai fait	aurons fait
feras	ferez	auras fait	aurez fait
fera	feront	aura fait	auront fait
Conditional		Conditional perfect	
ferais	ferions	aurais fait	aurions fait
ferais	feriez	aurais fait	auriez fait
ferait	feraient	aurait fait	auraient fait
Present subjunctive		Past subjunctive	
fasse	fassions	aie fait	ayons fait
fasses	fassiez	aies fait	ayez fait
fasse	fassent	ait fait	aient fait
Imperfect subjunctive		Pluperfect OR Past perfect subjunctive	
fisse	fissions	eusse fait	eussions fait
fisses	fissiez	eusses fait	eussiez fait
fît	fissent	eût fait	eussent fait
Imperative OR Command			
	fais		
	faisons		
	faites		

§7

§7.20 THREE REGULAR VERBS, FULLY CONJUGATED

The following regular verbs—*danser, finir,* and *vendre*—have been fully conjugated in all their tenses so that you can study regular *-er, -ir,* and *-re* verbs. For more fully conjugated verbs, along with exercises and answers explained, refer to *501 French Verbs,* also published by Barron's.

danser / to dance

Present participle: *dansant*   **Past participle: *dansé***

The Seven Simple Tenses		The Seven Compound Tenses	
Singular	**Plural**	**Singular**	**Plural**
Present indicative		Past indefinite (passé composé)	
danse	dansons	ai dansé	avons dansé
danses	dansez	as dansé	avez dansé
danse	dansent	a dansé	ont dansé
Imperfect indicative		Pluperfect OR Past perfect indicative	
dansais	dansions	avais dansé	avions dansé
dansais	dansiez	avais dansé	aviez dansé
dansait	dansaient	avait dansé	avaient dansé
Simple past		Past anterior	
dansai	dansâmes	eus dansé	eûmes dansé
dansas	dansâtes	eus dansé	eûtes dansé
dansa	dansèrent	eut dansé	eurent dansé
Future		Future perfect or Future anterior	
danserai	danserons	aurai dansé	aurons dansé
danseras	danserez	auras dansé	aurez dansé
dansera	danseront	aura dansé	auront dansé
Conditional		Conditional perfect	
danserais	danserions	aurais dansé	aurions dansé
danserais	danseriez	aurais dansé	auriez dansé
danserait	danseraient	aurait dansé	auraient dansé
Present subjunctive		Past subjunctive	
danse	dansions	aie dansé	ayons dansé
danses	dansiez	aies dansé	ayez dansé
danse	dansent	ait dansé	aient dansé
Imperfect subjunctive		Pluperfect or Past perfect subjunctive	
dansasse	dansassions	eusse dansé	eussions dansé
dansasses	dansassiez	eusses dansé	eussiez dansé
dansât	dansassent	eût dansé	eussent dansé
Imperative OR Command			
danse			
dansons			
dansez			

§7

finir / to finish
Present participle: *finissant*   **Past participle:** *fini*

The Seven Simple Tenses		The Seven Compound Tenses	
Singular	**Plural**	**Singular**	**Plural**
Present indicative		Past indefinite (passé composé)	
finis	*finissons*	*ai fini*	*avons fini*
finis	*finissez*	*as fini*	*avez fini*
finit	*finissent*	*a fini*	*ont fini*
Imperfect indicative		Pluperfect OR Past perfect indicative	
finissais	*finissions*	*avais fini*	*avions fini*
finissais	*finissiez*	*avais fini*	*aviez fini*
finissait	*finissaient*	*avait fini*	*avaient fini*
Simple past		Past anterior	
finis	*finîmes*	*eus fini*	*eûmes fini*
finis	*finîtes*	*eus fini*	*eûtes fini*
finit	*finirent*	*eut fini*	*eurent fini*
Future		Future perfect OR Future anterior	
finirai	*finirons*	*aurai fini*	*aurons fini*
finiras	*finirez*	*auras fini*	*aurez fini*
finira	*finiront*	*aura fini*	*auront fini*
Conditional		Conditional perfect	
finirais	*finirions*	*aurais fini*	*aurions fini*
finirais	*finiriez*	*aurais fini*	*auriez fini*
finirait	*finiraient*	*aurait fini*	*auraient fini*
Present subjunctive		Past subjunctive	
finisse	*finissions*	*aie fini*	*ayons fini*
finisses	*finissiez*	*aies fini*	*ayez fini*
finisse	*finissent*	*ait fini*	*aient fini*
Imperfect subjunctive		Pluperfect OR Past perfect subjunctive	
finisse	*finissions*	*eusse fini*	*eussions fini*
finisses	*finissiez*	*eusses fini*	*eussiez fini*
finît	*finissent*	*eût fini*	*eussent fini*

Imperative OR Command
finis
finissons
finissez

vendre / to sell

Present participle: *vendant* **Past participle:** *vendu*

The Seven Simple Tenses		The Seven Compound Tenses	
Singular	**Plural**	**Singular**	**Plural**
Present indicative		Past indefinite (passé composé)	
vends	*vendons*	*ai vendu*	*avons vendu*
vends	*vendez*	*as vendu*	*avez vendu*
vend	*vendent*	*a vendu*	*ont vendu*
Imperfect indicative		Pluperfect OR Past perfect indicative	
vendais	*vendions*	*avais vendu*	*avions vendu*
vendais	*vendiez*	*avais vendu*	*aviez vendu*
vendait	*vendaient*	*avait vendu*	*avaient vendu*
Simple past		Past anterior	
vendis	*vendîmes*	*eus vendu*	*eûmes vendu*
vendis	*vendîtes*	*eus vendu*	*eûtes vendu*
vendit	*vendirent*	*eut vendu*	*eurent vendu*
Future		Future perfect OR Future anterior	
vendrai	*vendrons*	*aurai vendu*	*aurons vendu*
vendras	*vendrez*	*auras vendu*	*aurez vendu*
vendra	*vendront*	*aura vendu*	*auront vendu*
Conditional		Conditional perfect	
vendrais	*vendrions*	*aurais vendu*	*aurions vendu*
vendrais	*vendriez*	*aurais vendu*	*auriez vendu*
vendrait	*vendraient*	*aurait vendu*	*auraient vendu*
Present subjunctive		Past subjunctive	
vende	*vendions*	*aie vendu*	*ayons vendu*
vendes	*vendiez*	*aies vendu*	*ayez vendu*
vende	*vendent*	*ait vendu*	*aient vendu*
Imperfect subjunctive		Pluperfect or Past perfect subjunctive	
vendisse	*vendissions*	*eusse vendu*	*eussions vendu*
vendisses	*vendissiez*	*eusses vendu*	*eussiez vendu*
vendît	*vendissent*	*eût vendu*	*eussent vendu*

Imperative OR Command

vends

vendons

vendez

§7

Summary of verb tenses and moods in French with English equivalent

Les Sept Temps Simples *The Seven Simple Tenses*		Les Sept Temps Composés *The Seven Compound Tenses*	
Tense No.	Tense Name	Tense No.	Tense Name
1	**Présent de l'indicatif** *Present indicative*	8	**Passé composé** *Past indefinite or Compound past*
2	**Imparfait de l'indicatif** *Imperfect indicative*	9	**Plus-que-parfait de l'indicatif** *Pluperfect indicative*
3	**Passé simple** *Past definite or Simple past*	10	**Passé antérieur** *Past anterior*
4	**Futur** *Future*	11	**Futur antérieur** *Future perfect*
5	**Conditionnel** *Conditional*	12	**Conditionnel passé** *Condixtional perfect*
6	**Présent du subjonctif** *Present subjunctive*	13	**Passé du subjonctif** *Past subjunctive*
7	**Imparfait du subjonctif** *Imperfect subjunctive*	14	**Plus-que-parfait du subjonctif** *Pluperfect subjunctive*

The imperative is not a tense; it is a mood.

§8.

Adverbs

DEFINITION

An *adverb* is a word that modifies a verb, an adjective, or
another adverb.

§8.1 FORMATION

Many French adverbs are not formed from another word; for
example: *bien, mal, vite, combien, comment, pourquoi, où.*

There are many other adverbs that are formed from
another word. The usual way is to add the suffix *-ment* to the
masculine singular form of an adjective whose last letter is a
vowel; for example: *probable, probablement; poli, poliment;
vrai, vraiment.*

The suffix *-ment* is added to the feminine singular form
if the masculine singular ends in a consonant; for example:
*affreux, affreuse, affreusement; seul, seule, seulement; amer,
amère, amèrement; franc, franche, franchement.*

The ending *-ment* is equivalent to the English ending "-ly":
lent, lente, lentement / slow, slowly.

Some adjectives that end in *-ant* or *-ent* become
adverbs by changing *-ant* to *-amment* and *-ent* to *-emment*:
*innocent, innocemment; constant, constamment; récent,
récemment.*

Some adverbs take *é* instead of *e* before adding *-ment*:
*profond, profondément; confus, confusément; précis,
précisément.*

The adjective *gentil* becomes *gentiment* as an adverb and
bref becomes *brièvement.*

§8

145

§8.2 POSITION

> 1. *David aime beaucoup les chocolats.*
> 2. *Paulette a parlé distinctement.*
> 3. *Julie a bien parlé.*

- In French, an adverb ordinarily follows the simple verb it modifies, as in the first model sentence above.
- If a verb is compound, as in the *past indefinite* (sentence 2), the adverb generally follows the past participle if it is a long adverb. The adverb *distinctement* is long. Some exceptions: *certainement*, *complètement*, and *probablement* are usually placed between the helping verb and the past participle: *Elle est probablement partie. Il a complètement fini le travail.*
- If a verb is compound, as in the *past indefinite* (sentence 3), short common adverbs (like *beaucoup, bien, déjà, encore, mal, mieux, souvent, toujours*) ordinarily precede the past participle; in other words, they may be placed between the helping verb and the past participle.
- For emphasis, an adverb may be placed at the beginning of a sentence: *Malheureusement, Suzanne est déjà partie.*

§8.3 TYPES

§8.3–1 Interrogative Adverbs

Some common interrogative adverbs are *comment, combien, pourquoi, quand, où.*

Examples:
Comment allez-vous? Combien coûte ce livre? Pourquoi partez-vous? Quand arriverez-vous? Où allez-vous?

§8.3–2 Adverbs of Quantity

Some adverbial expressions of quantity are *beaucoup de*, *assez de, peu de, trop de, plus de*. With these, no article is used: *peu de sucre, beaucoup de travail, assez de temps, trop de lait, combien d'argent*.

§8.3–3 Comparative and Superlative Adverbs

Adverb	Comparative	Superlative
vite / quickly	*plus vite (que) /* more quickly (than) faster (than)	*le plus vite /* (the) most quickly, (the) fastest
	moins vite (que) / less quickly (than)	*le moins vite /* (the) least quickly
	aussi vite (que) / as quickly (as), as fast (as)	

Examples:

Arlette parle plus vite que Marie-France. / Arlette speaks faster than Marie-France.

Madame Legrange parle moins vite que Madame Duval. / Madame Legrange speaks less quickly than Madame Duval.

Monsieur Bernard parle aussi vite que Monsieur Claude. / Monsieur Bernard speaks as fast as Monsieur Claude.

Madame Durocher parle le plus vite tandis que Madame Milot parle le moins vite. / Madame Durocher speaks the fastest whereas Madame Milot speaks the least fast (the slowest).

Aussi . . . que should become si . . . que in a negative sentence. However, native speakers do not always make this change. See also §5.4–5.

§8

Example:
Justin ne parle pas si vite que Justine. / Justin does not talk as fast as Justine.

Irregular Comparative and Superlative Adverb

Adverb	Comparative	Superlative
bien / well	*mieux* / better	*le mieux* / best, the best
beaucoup / much	*plus* / more	*le plus* / most, the most
mal / badly	*plus mal* / worse *pis* / worse	*le plus mal* / worst, the worst *le moins bien* / the worst *le pis* / worst, the worst
peu / little	*moins* / less	*le moins* / least, the least

Examples:
Pierre travaille bien, Henri travaille mieux que Robert et Georges travaille le mieux.

Marie étudie beaucoup, Paulette étudie plus que Marie, et Henriette étudie le plus.

§8.4 *OUI* AND *SI*

Ordinarily, *oui* is used to mean "yes." However, *si* can also be used to mean "yes" in response to a question in the negative.

Examples:
Aimez-vous le français?—Oui, j'aime le français.
N'aimez-vous pas le français?—Si, j'aime le français.

Tip	*Une scie* (pronounced like the English "see") is a carpenter's "saw." Seesaw!

§9.

Prepositions—Special Uses

§9.1 *DANS* AND *EN* + A LENGTH OF TIME

The prepositions *dans* and *en* both mean "in," but each is used in a different sense.

Dans + a length of time indicates that something will happen *at the end* of that length of time.

Le docteur va venir dans une demi-heure. / The doctor will come in a half-hour (*i.e.,* at the end of a half-hour).

Dans and a duration of time can be at the beginning of the sentence or at the end of it and future time is ordinarily implied.

En + a length of time indicates that something happened or will happen at any time *within* that length of time.

Examples:

Robert a fait cela en une heure. / Robert did that in (within) an (one) hour.

Robert fera cela en une heure. / Robert will do that in (within) an (one) hour.

BUT

Robert fera cela dans une heure. / Robert will do that in (at the end of) an (one) hour.

 Tip — To remember that *dans* indicates at the end of an hour, note that *dans* and **end** both have a **d** in them.

§9.2 *ENVERS* AND *VERS*

Envers is used in a figurative sense in the meaning of "with regard to" someone, "with respect to" someone, "for" someone, or "for" something.

149

Example:
Je montre beaucoup de respect envers les vieilles personnes. /
I show a lot of respect toward old persons.

Vers also means "toward," but is used in the physical sense
(in the direction of) as well as in the figurative sense.

Examples:
Pourquoi allez-vous vers la porte? / Why are you going toward the
door?
Je vais partir vers trois heures. / I am going to leave toward
(around) three o'clock.

§9.3 *PENDANT*

IN THE PRESENT TENSE

Combien de temps étudiez-vous chaque soir? / How long do you
study every evening?
J'étudie une heure chaque soir. / I study one hour each night. OR
J'étudie pendant une heure chaque soir. / I study for one hour
each night.

IN THE PAST INDEFINITE

Combien de temps êtes-vous resté(e) à Paris? / How long did you
stay in Paris?
Je suis resté(e) à Paris deux semaines. / I stayed in Paris two
weeks. OR *Je suis resté(e) à Paris pendant deux semaines.* /
I stayed in Paris for two weeks.

IN THE FUTURE

Combien de temps resterez-vous à Paris? / How long will you stay
in Paris?
J'y resterai pendant deux semaines. / I will stay there for two
weeks. OR *J'y resterai deux semaines.* / I will stay there two
weeks.

§10.

Conjunctions

§10.1 DEFINITION

A conjunction is a word that connects words, phrases, clauses, or sentences, such as *et* / and, *mais* / but, *ou* / or, *parce que* / because. The following is a list of the most common conjunctions.

§10.2 BASIC CONJUNCTIONS

Review §7.15, the Subjunctive after Certain Conjunctions.

à moins que / unless
afin que / in order that, so that
aussitôt que / as soon as
avant que / before
bien que / although
car / for
comme / as, since
de crainte que / for fear that
de peur que / for fear that
de sorte que / so that, in such a way that
depuis que / since
dès que / as soon as
donc / therefore, consequently
en même temps que / at the same time as
et / and
jusqu'à ce que / until
lorsque / when, at the time when
maintenant que / now that
mais / but
ou / or
parce que / because
pendant le temps que / while
pendant que / while
pour que / in order that
pourvu que / provided that

puisque / since
quand / when
que / that
quoi que / whatever, no matter what
quoique / although
si / if
tandis que / while, whereas
vu que / seeing (that), considering (that)

Tip	Pronounce the final *c* in *donc* as a *k* when it means consequently (therefore).

Je pense; donc, je suis, I think; therefore, I am.

Examples:

Nous vous permettons d'entrer, pourvu que vous payiez le droit d'entrée. / We (will) allow you to enter, provided that you pay the entry fee.

Je t'enverrai un texto dès que j'arriverai à la gare. / I'll text you as soon as I arrive at the station.

Special Topics

§11.

Order of Elements in French Sentences

§11.1 REVIEW OF NEGATIVE CONSTRUCTIONS

Please review §7.18 before studying the following sections.

§11.2 DECLARATIVE SENTENCE WITH A VERB IN A SIMPLE TENSE (*e.g.*, PRESENT)

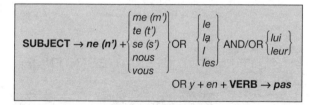

$$\text{SUBJECT} \rightarrow ne\ (n') + \begin{Bmatrix} me\ (m') \\ te\ (t') \\ se\ (s') \\ nous \\ vous \end{Bmatrix} \text{OR} \begin{Bmatrix} le \\ la \\ l' \\ les \end{Bmatrix} \text{AND/OR} \begin{Bmatrix} lui \\ leur \end{Bmatrix}$$

$$\text{OR } y + en + \textbf{VERB} \rightarrow \textit{pas}$$

Examples:
Il ne me les donne pas. / He is not giving them to me.
Je ne le leur donne pas. / I am not giving it to them.
Il n'y en a pas. / There aren't any of them.

§11.3 DECLARATIVE SENTENCE WITH A VERB IN A COMPOUND TENSE (*e.g.,* ***PASSÉ COMPOSÉ***)

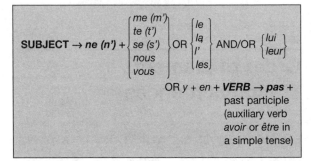

SUBJECT → *ne (n')* +
$\begin{cases} me\ (m') \\ te\ (t') \\ se\ (s') \\ nous \\ vous \end{cases}$
OR
$\begin{cases} le \\ la \\ l' \\ les \end{cases}$
AND/OR
$\begin{cases} lui \\ leur \end{cases}$

OR *y + en* + **VERB** → *pas* + past participle (auxiliary verb *avoir* or être in a simple tense)

Examples:

Yvonne ne s'est pas lavée. / Yvonne did not wash herself.

Il ne m'en a pas envoyé. / He did not send any of them to me.

Je ne le lui ai pas donné. / I did not give it to him (to her).

Nous ne vous les avons pas données. / We have not given them to you.

Ils ne s'en sont pas allés. / They did not go away. *(s'en aller* / to go away)

§11.4 AFFIRMATIVE IMPERATIVE SENTENCE

VERB +
$\begin{cases} le \\ la \\ l' \\ les \end{cases}$
OR
$\begin{cases} moi\ (m') \\ toi\ (t') \\ nous \\ vous \end{cases}$
AND/OR
$\begin{cases} lui \\ leur \end{cases}$
OR *y + en*

Examples:

Donnez-les-leur. / Give them to them.
Assieds-toi. / Sit down.
Allez-vous-en! / Go away!
Apportez-le-moi! / Bring it to me!
Donnez-m'en! / Give me some!
Allez-y! / Go to it! Go there!

§11.5 NEGATIVE IMPERATIVE SENTENCE

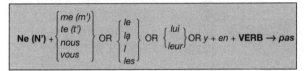

$$\text{Ne (N')} + \begin{Bmatrix} me\ (m') \\ te\ (t') \\ nous \\ vous \end{Bmatrix} \text{OR} \begin{Bmatrix} le \\ la \\ l \\ les \end{Bmatrix} \text{OR} \begin{Bmatrix} lui \\ leur \end{Bmatrix} \text{OR } y + en + \textbf{VERB} \rightarrow pas$$

Examples:

Ne l'y mettez pas. / Do not put it in it. Do not put it there.
Ne les leur donnez pas. / Do not give them to them.
Ne t'assieds pas! / Don't sit down!
Ne vous en allez pas! / Don't go away!

 Tip   Object pronouns fall in the right order if you
alphabetize them!

$$\left. \begin{array}{c} la \\ le \\ les \end{array} \right\} + \begin{array}{c} leur \\ lui \end{array} \\ +$$

The order is always the same, whether before or
after a verb or before an infinitive.

§12.

Idioms and Idiomatic Expressions

§12.1 SPECIAL USES

Depuis

• With the present indicative tense

When an action of some sort began in the past and is still going on in the present, use the present tense with *depuis* + the length of time.

Je travaille dans ce bureau depuis trois ans. / I have been working in this office for three years.

> **Tip** Use *depuis combien de temps* + the present indicative of the verb to ask how long one has been + verb: *Depuis combien de temps travaillez-vous dans ce bureau?* / How long have you been working in this office? *Je travaille dans ce bureau depuis un an.* / I have been working in this office for one year.

• With the imperfect indicative tense

When an action of some sort began in the past and continued up to another point in the past that you are telling about, use the imperfect indicative tense with *depuis* + the length of time:

J'attendais l'autobus depuis vingt minutes quand il est arrivé. / I had been waiting for the bus for twenty minutes when it arrived.

• In a question

> *Depuis combien de temps attendez-vous l'autobus?* / How long
>   have you been waiting for the bus?
> *J'attends l'autobus depuis vingt minutes.* / I have been waiting for
>   the bus for twenty minutes.

Tip	Note: When you use *depuis combien de temps* in a question, you expect the other person to tell you how long, how much time—how many minutes, how many hours, how many days, weeks, months, years, etc.

> *Depuis quand habitez-vous cet appartement?* / Since when have
>   you been living in this apartment?
> *J'habite cet appartement depuis le premier septembre.* / I have
>   been living in this apartment since September first.

Tip	Note: When you use *depuis quand* in your question, you expect the other person to tell you since what particular point in time in the past—a particular day, date, month; in other words, since *when*, not *how long*.

> *Depuis quand êtes-vous malade?* / Since when have you been
>   sick?
> *Je suis malade depuis samedi.* / I have been sick since Saturday.
> *Depuis quand habitiez-vous l'appartement quand vous avez
>   déménagé?* / Since when had you been living in the apartment
>   when you moved?
> *J'habitais l'appartement depuis le cinq avril dernier quand j'ai
>   déménagé.* / I had been living in the apartment since last April
>   fifth when I moved.

Il y a + Length of Time + *que; voici* + Length of Time + *que; voilà* + Length of Time + *que*

• In questions and answers

> *Depuis combien de temps attendez-vous l'autobus?* / How long
>   have you been waiting for the bus?

J'attends l'autobus depuis vingt minutes. / I have been waiting for
the bus for twenty minutes.

Voici vingt minutes que je l'attends. / I have been waiting for it for
twenty minutes.

Voilà vingt minutes que je l'attends. / I have been waiting for it for
twenty minutes.

Il y a vingt minutes que je l'attends. / I have been waiting for it for
twenty minutes.

Ça fait vingt minutes que je l'attends. / I have been waiting for it for
twenty minutes.

| Tip | Note: When you use these expressions, you generally use them at the beginning of your answer + the verb. When you use the *depuis* construction, the verb comes first: *J'attends l'autobus depuis vingt minutes.* |

• *Il y a* + length of time

Il y a + length of time means "ago." Do not use *que* in this
construction as in the above examples because the meaning
is entirely different.

Madame Martin est partie il y a une heure. / Mrs. Martin left an
hour ago.

L'autobus est arrivé il y a vingt minutes. / The bus arrived twenty
minutes ago.

Il y a and *Il y avait* when not talking about time

• *Il y a* and *Il y avait*

Il y a alone means "there is" or "there are" when you are
merely making a statement.

Il y a vingt élèves dans cette classe. / There are twenty students in
this class.

Il y a une mouche dans la soupe. / There is a fly in the soup.

Il y avait alone means "there was" or "there were" when you
are merely making a statement.

Il y avait vingt élèves dans cette classe. / There were (used to be)
twenty students in this class.

Il y avait deux mouches dans la soupe. / There were two flies in
the soup.

When you use *il y a* and *il y avait* in the negative, remember to use *de* instead of an indefinite article. (See §3.3, Simple Negative.)

> *Il n'y a pas de lait dans le frigo.* / There isn't any milk in the refrigerator.
> *Il n'y avait pas de clients dans le magasin.* / There weren't any customers in the store.

Voici and *Voilà*

These two expressions are used to point out someone or something.

> *Voici un taxi!* / Here's a taxi!
> *Voilà un taxi là-bas!* / There's a taxi over there!
> *Voici ma carte d'identité et voilà mon passeport.* / Here's my ID card and there's my passport.
> *Voici mon père et voilà ma mère.* / Here's my father and there's my mother.

§12.2 BASIC EXPRESSIONS, BEGINNER AND INTERMEDIATE LEVELS

With *à*

à bicyclette / by bicycle, on a bicycle	*à droite* / at (on, to) the right
à bientôt / so long, see you soon	*à gauche* / at (on, to) the left
à bord / aboard, on board	*à haute voix* / aloud, out loud, in a loud voice
à cause de / on account of, because of	*à jamais* / forever
à cette heure / at this time, at the present moment	*à l'école* / at (in, to) school
à cheval / on horseback	*à l'étranger* / abroad, overseas
à côté de / beside, next to	*à l'heure* / on time
à demain / until tomorrow, see you tomorrow	*à l'instant* / instantly

à l'occasion / on the occasion

à la campagne / at (in, to) the country(side)

à la fin / at last, finally

à la fois / at the same time

à la main / in one's hand, by hand

à la maison / at home

à la mode / fashionable, in style, in fashion

à la radio / on the radio

à la recherche de / in search of

à la télé / on TV

à mon avis / in my opinion

à part / aside

à partir de / beginning with

à peine / hardly, scarcely

à peu près / approximately, about, nearly

à pied / on foot

à plus tard / see you later

à présent / now, at present

à propos / by the way

à propos de / about, with reference to, concerning

à quelle heure? / at what time?

à qui est ce livre? / whose is this book?

à quoi bon? / what's the use?

à son gré / to one's liking

à temps / in time

à tour de rôle / in turn

à tout à l'heure / see you in a little while

à tout prix / at any cost

à travers / across, through

à tue-tête / at the top of one's voice, as loud as possible

à vélo / on a bike

à voix basse / in a low voice, softly

à volonté / at will, willingly

à vrai dire / to tell the truth

à vue d'œil / visibly

With *au*

au bas de / at the bottom of

au besoin / if need be, if necessary

au bout de / at the end of, at the tip of

au contraire / on the contrary

au début / at (in) the beginning

au-dessous de / below, beneath

au-dessus de / above, over

au fond de / at the bottom of

au sommet de / at the top of
au lieu de / instead of
au milieu de / in the middle of
au moins / at least
au pied de / at the foot of
au printemps / in the spring (but *en automne, en hiver, en été*)
au revoir / goodbye

au sous-sol / in the basement
au sujet de / about, concerning
au téléphone / on the telephone
café au lait / coffee with milk
rosbif au jus / roast beef with gravy

With *aux*

aux dépens / at the expense
aux (pommes) frites / with French fries

rire aux éclats / to roar with laughter
sauter aux yeux / to be evident, self-evident

With *aller*

aller / to feel (health): *Comment allez-vous?*
aller à / to be becoming, fit, suit: *Cette robe lui va bien.* / This dress suits her fine. *Sa barbe ne lui va pas.* / His beard does not look good on him.
aller à la chasse / to go hunting
aller à la pêche / to go fishing

aller à la rencontre de quelqu'un / to go to meet someone
aller à pied / to walk, go on foot
aller au fond des choses / to get to the bottom of things
aller chercher / to go get
allons donc! / nonsense! come on, now!

With *avoir*

§12

avoir . . . ans / to
be . . . years old: *Quel âge
avez-vous?* / J'ai dix-sept
ans.
avoir à + infinitive / to have to
avoir affaire à quelqu'un / to
deal with someone
avoir beau + infinitive / to
be useless + infinitive,
to do something in vain:
*Vous avez beau parler;
je ne vous écoute pas.* /
You are talking in vain; I
am not listening to you.
avoir besoin de / to need, to
have need of
avoir bonne mine / to look
well
avoir chaud / to be (feel)
warm (persons)
avoir congé / to have a day
off, a holiday
avoir de la chance / to be
lucky
avoir de quoi + infinitive / to
have the material, means,
enough + infinitive: *As-tu
de quoi manger?* / Have
you something (enough)
to eat?
avoir des nouvelles / to
receive news
avoir du savoir-faire / to
have tact

avoir du savoir-vivre / to
have good manners
avoir envie de + infinitive /
to have a desire to
avoir faim / to be (feel) hungry
avoir froid / to be (feel) cold
(persons)
avoir hâte / to be in a hurry
avoir honte / to be
ashamed, to feel
ashamed
avoir l'air + adjective / to
seem, to look + adjective:
Vous avez l'air malade. /
You look sick. (The
adjective can agree with
either *air* or the subject.
*Madeleine a l'air con-
tente.* or *Madeleine a l'air
content.*)
avoir l'air de + infinitive / to
appear + infinitive: *Vous
avez l'air d'être malade.* /
You appear to be sick.
avoir l'habitude de + infinitive / to be accustomed
to, to be in the habit of:
*J'ai l'habitude de faire
mes devoirs avant le
dîner.* / I'm in the habit
of doing my homework
before dinner.

avoir l'idée de + infinitive / to have a notion + infinitive

avoir l'intention de + infinitive / to intend + infinitive

avoir la bonté de + infinitive / to have the kindness

avoir la langue bien pendue / to have the gift of gab

avoir la parole / to have the floor (to speak)

avoir le cœur gros / to be heartbroken

avoir le temps de + infinitive / to have (the) time + infinitive

avoir lieu / to take place

avoir mal / to feel sick

avoir mal à + (place where it hurts) / to have a pain or ache in . . . : *J'ai mal à la jambe.* / My leg hurts. *J'ai mal au dos.* / My back hurts. *J'ai mal au cou.* / I have a pain in the neck.

avoir mauvaise mine / to look ill, not to look well

avoir peine à + infinitive / to have difficulty in + present participle

avoir peur de / to be afraid of

avoir pitié de / to take pity on

avoir raison / to be right (persons)

avoir soif / to be thirsty

avoir sommeil / to be sleepy

avoir son mot à dire / to have one's way

avoir tort / to be wrong (persons)

avoir une faim de loup / to be starving

With *bas*

au bas de / at the bottom of
en bas / downstairs, below
là-bas / over there
A bas les devoirs! / Down with homework!

parler tout bas / to speak very softly
de haut en bas / from top to bottom

With *bien*

§12

aller bien / to be well

bien des / many: *Roger a bien des amis.* / Roger has many friends.

bien entendu / of course

dire du bien de / to speak well of

être bien aise / to be very glad, happy

tant bien que mal / rather badly, so-so

bien sûr / of course

Tip

In response to the question, "*Comment all-ez-vous?* / How are you?" you should answer, "*Je vais bien* / I'm well" or "*Bien* / Fine" and not "*Je suis bien.*" If the question uses the verb *aller*, remember to answer with *aller*, even though you may use the verb **to be** in English; in this situation, *bien* is an adverb. (See page 170, *être bien.*)

With *bon*

à quoi bon? / what's the use?

bon gré, mal gré / willing or not, willy nilly

bon marché / cheap, at a low price

bon pour quelqu'un / good for someone

de bon appétit / with good appetite, heartily

de bon cœur / gladly, willingly

savoir bon gré à quelqu'un / to be thankful, grateful to someone

With *ça*

çà et là / here and there

Ça m'est égal. / It makes no difference to me.

Ça m'énerve! / That annoys me!

Ça va? / Is everything okay?

Ça y est. / That's it.

C'est comme ça! / That's how it is!

comme ci, comme ça / so-so

Pas de ça! / None of that!

With *cela*

Cela est égal. / It's all the same. It doesn't matter. It makes no difference.

Cela m'est égal. / It doesn't matter to me. It's all the same to me.

Cela n'importe. / That doesn't matter.

Cela ne fait rien. / That makes no difference.

Cela ne sert à rien. / That serves no purpose.

Cela ne vous regarde pas. / That's none of your business.

malgré cela / in spite of that

malgré tout cela / in spite of all that

Qu'est-ce que cela veut dire? / What does that mean?

With *ce, c'est, est-ce*

c'est-à-dire / that is, that is to say

C'est aujourd'hui lundi. / Today is Monday.

C'est dommage. / It's a pity. It's too bad.

C'est entendu. / It's understood. It's agreed. All right. OK.

C'est épatant! / It's wonderful!

C'est trop fort! / That's just too much!

n'est-ce pas? / isn't that so? isn't it?, etc.

Qu'est-ce que c'est? / What is it?

Quel jour est-ce aujourd'hui? / What day is it today? *C'est lundi.* / It's Monday.

Qu'est-ce qui s'est passé? / What happened?

With *d'*

changer d'avis / to change one's opinion, one's mind

comme d'habitude / as usual

d'abord / at first

d'accord / okay, agreed

d'ailleurs / besides, moreover

d'aujourd'hui en huit / a week from today

d'avance / in advance, beforehand

d'habitude / ordinarily, usually, generally

d'ici longtemps / for a long time to come

d'ordinaire / ordinarily, usually, generally

tout d'un coup / all of a sudden

With *de*

au sommet de / at the top of

autour de / around

changer de train / to change trains: *changer de vêtements* / to change clothes

combien de / how much, how many

de bon appétit / with good appetite, heartily

de bon cœur / gladly, willingly

de bonne heure / early

de cette façon / in this way

de jour en jour / from day to day

de l'autre côté de / on the other side of

de la part de / on behalf of, from

de nouveau / again

de parti pris / on purpose, deliberately

de plus / furthermore

de plus en plus / more and more

de quelle couleur . . . ? / what color . . . ?

de quoi + infinitive / something, enough + infinitive: *de quoi écrire* / something to write with; *de quoi manger* / something or enough to eat; *de quoi vivre* / something or enough to live on

de rien / you're welcome, don't mention it

de rigueur / required, obligatory

de son mieux / one's best

de suite / one after another, in succession

de temps en temps / from time to time, occasionally

de toutes ses forces / with all one's might, strenuously

du côté de / in the direction of, toward

éclater de rire / to burst out laughing

en face de / opposite

entendre parler de / to hear about

être de retour / to be back

être en train de / to be in the act of, in the process of

être temps de + infinitive / to be time + infinitive

faire semblant de + infinitive / to pretend + infinitive

féliciter quelqu'un de quelque chose / to congratulate someone for something

Il n'y a pas de quoi! / You're welcome!

jamais de la vie! / never in one's life! never! out of the question!

jouer de / to play (a musical instrument)

manquer de + infinitive / to fail to, to almost do something: *Victor a manqué de se noyer.* / Victor almost drowned.

mettre de côté / to lay aside, to save

pas de mal! / no harm!

près de / near

quelque chose de + adjective / something + adjective: *J'ai bu quelque chose de bon!* / I drank something good!

Quoi de neuf? / What's new?

Rien de neuf! / Nothing's new!

tout de même / all the same

tout de suite / immediately, at once

venir de + infinitive / to have just done something; *Je viens de manger.* / I have just eaten.

With *du*

dire du bien de quelqu'un / to speak well of someone

dire du mal de quelqu'un / to speak ill of someone

donner du chagrin à quelqu'un / to give someone grief

du côté de / in the direction of, toward

du matin au soir / from morning until night

du moins / at least

du reste / besides, in addition, furthermore

montrer du doigt / to point out, to show, to indicate by pointing

pas du tout / not at all

With *en*

de jour en jour / from day to day

de temps en temps / from time to time

en anglais, en français, etc. / in English, in French, etc.

en arrière / backwards, to the rear, behind

en automne, en hiver, en été / in the fall, in winter, in summer (But "in the springtime" is *au printemps*.)

en automobile / by car

en avion / by plane

en avoir plein le dos / to be sick and tired of something

en bas / downstairs, below

en bateau / by boat

en bois, en pierre, en + a material / made of wood, of stone, etc.

en chemin de fer / by train

en dessous (de) / underneath

en dessus (de) / above, on top, over

en effet / in fact, indeed, yes, indeed

en face de / opposite

en famille / as a family

en haut / upstairs, above

en huit jours / in a week

en même temps / at the same time

en panne / broken down, out of order

en plein air / in the open air, outdoors
en retard / late, not on time
en tout cas / in any case, at any rate
en toute hâte / with all possible speed, haste
en ville / downtown, in (at, to) town
En voilà assez! / Enough of that!
en voiture / by car: *en voiture!* / all aboard!

être en train de + infinitive / to be in the act of + present participle, to be in the process of, to be busy + present participle
Je vous en prie. / I beg you. You're welcome.
mettre en pièces / to tear to pieces, to break into pieces
voir tout en rose / to see the bright side of things, to be optimistic

With *être*

être à l'heure / to be on time
être à quelqu'un / to belong to someone: *Ce livre est à moi.* / This book belongs to me.
être au courant de / to be informed about
être bien / to be comfortable, good
être d'accord avec / to agree with
être de retour / to be back
être en retard / to be late, not to be on time

être en train de + infinitive / to be in the act of, to be in the process of, to be busy + present participle
être en vacances / to be on vacation
être enrhumé / to have a cold, be sick with a cold
être pressé(e) / to be in a hurry
Quelle heure est-il? / What time is it? *Il est une heure.* / It is one o'clock. *Il est deux heures.* / It is two o'clock.

Tip

Do not confuse *être bien* with *aller bien*. (See *aller bien*, page 165.)
Tu veux changer de place? / Do you want to change seats?
Non, merci, je suis bien. / No, thank you, I'm good (I'm comfortable).

With *faire*

Cela ne fait rien. / That doesn't matter.

Comment se fait-il? / How come?

faire à sa tête / to have one's way

faire attention (à) / to pay attention (to)

faire beau / to be pleasant, nice weather

faire bon accueil / to welcome

faire chaud / to be warm (weather)

faire de l'autostop / to hitchhike

faire de son mieux / to do one's best

faire des châteaux en Espagne / to build castles in the air

faire des emplettes; faire des courses; faire du shopping / to do or to go shopping

faire des progrès / to make progress

faire du bien à quelqu'un / to do good for someone

faire du lèche-vitrines / to go window-shopping

faire du vélo / to ride a bike

faire exprès / to do on purpose

faire face à / to oppose, to face, to face up to

faire froid / to be cold (weather)

faire jour / to be daylight

faire la bête / to act like a fool

faire la connaissance de quelqu'un / to make the acquaintance of someone, meet someone for the first time

faire la cuisine / to do the cooking

faire la grasse matinée / to sleep late in the morning

faire la lessive / to do the laundry

faire (une) la malle / to pack (a) the trunk

faire la queue / to line up, to get in line, to stand in line

faire la vaisselle / to do (wash) the dishes

faire le ménage / to do housework

faire les bagages / to pack the baggage, luggage

faire les valises / to pack the suitcases, valises

faire mal à quelqu'un / to hurt, to harm someone

faire nuit / to be night(time)

faire peur à quelqu'un / to frighten someone

faire plaisir à quelqu'un / to please someone

faire sa toilette / to wash and dress oneself

faire ses adieux / to say goodbye

faire son possible / to do one's best

faire suivre le courrier / to forward mail

faire un tour / to go for a stroll

faire un voyage / to take a trip

faire une partie de / to play a game of

faire une promenade / to take a walk

faire une visite / to pay a visit

faire venir quelqu'un / to have someone come: *Il a fait venir le docteur.* / He had the doctor come.

faire venir l'eau à la bouche / to make one's mouth water

Faites comme chez vous! / Make yourself at home!

Que faire? / What is to be done?

Quel temps fait-il? / What's the weather like?

With *mieux*

aimer mieux / to prefer, like better

aller mieux / to feel better (person's health): *Êtes-vous toujours malade?* / Are you still sick? *Je vais mieux, merci.* / I'm feeling better, thank you.

au mieux / at best

de mieux en mieux / better and better

de son mieux / one's best

faire de son mieux / to do one's best

tant mieux / so much the better

valoir mieux / to be better (worth more), to be preferable

§12

With *non*

Je crois que non. / I don't think so.
Mais non! / Of course not!

Non merci! / No, thank you!
J'espère bien que non. / I hope not.

With *par*

par bonheur / fortunately
par-ci par-là / here and there
par conséquent / consequently, therefore
par-dessous / under(neath)
par-dessus / over (the top of)
par exemple / for example
par hasard / by chance
par ici / through here, this way, in this direction
par jour / per day, daily
par la fenêtre / out, through the window
par-là / through there, that way, in that direction

par malheur / unfortunately
par mois / per month, monthly
par semaine / per week, weekly
par tous les temps / in all kinds of weather
apprendre par cœur / to learn by heart, memorize
finir par + infinitive / to end up + present participle: *Ils ont fini par se marier.* / They ended up by getting married.
jeter l'argent par la fenêtre / to waste money

With *plus*

de plus / furthermore, besides, in addition
de plus en plus / more and more
n'en pouvoir plus / to be exhausted, not to be able to go on any longer: *Je n'en peux plus!* / I can't go on any longer!

Plus ça change plus c'est la même chose. / The more it changes, the more it remains the same.
une fois de plus / once more, one more time

With *quel*

Quel âge avez-vous? / How old are you? *Quel garçon!* / What a boy!	*Quel jour est-ce aujourd'hui?* / What day is it today?

With *quelle*

De quelle couleur est (sont) . . . ? / What color is (are) . . . ? *Quelle fille!* / What a girl!	*Quelle heure est-il?* / What time is it? *Quelle chance!* / What luck!

With *quelque chose*

quelque chose à + infinitive / something + infinitive: *J'ai quelque chose à lui dire.* / I have something to say to him (to her).	*quelque chose de* + adjective / something + adjective: *J'ai quelque chose d'intéressant à vous dire.* / I have something interesting to tell you.

With *quoi*

à quoi bon? / what's the use? *avoir de quoi* + infinitive / to have something (enough) + infinitive: *Avez-vous de quoi écrire?* / Do you have something to write with?	*avoir de quoi manger* / to have something to eat *Il n'y a pas de quoi!* / You're welcome! *Quoi!* / What! *Quoi?* / What? *Quoi de neuf?* / What's new?

Example:
Quoi? Je n'ai pas entendu ce que tu as dit. / What? I didn't hear what you said.

With *rien*

Cela ne fait rien. / That doesn't matter.	*Rien de neuf!* / Nothing's new!
Cela ne sert à rien. / That serves no purpose.	*rien de rien* / nothing at all
de rien / you're welcome, don't mention it	*rien du tout* / nothing at all

Example:
Je n'ai rien dans la poche, rien de rien. / I have nothing in my pocket, nothing at all.

With *tant*

tant bien que mal / so-so	*Je t'aime tant!* / I love you so much!
tant mieux / so much the better	*tant de choses* / so many things
tant pis / so much the worse	
J'ai tant de travail! / I have so much work!	

With *tous*

tous (les) deux / both (m. plural)	*tous les matins* / every morning
tous les ans / every year	*tous les soirs* / every evening
tous les jours / every day	*tous les mois* / every month

With *tout*

après tout / after all	*tout d'abord* / first of all
en tout cas / in any case, at any rate	*tout d'un coup* / all of a sudden, all at once
pas du tout / not at all	*tout de même!* / all the same! just the same!
tout à coup / suddenly	*tout de suite* / immediately, at once, right away
tout à fait / completely, entirely	
tout à l'heure / a little while ago, in a little while	*tout le monde* / everybody
	tout le temps / all the time

With *toute*

en toute connaissance de cause / knowing all the facts	*de toutes ses forces* / with all one's might
en toute hâte / with all possible speed, in great haste	*toutes (les) deux* / both (f. plural)
toute chose / everything	*toutes les nuits* / every night

With *y*

Allez-y! (polite) or *Vas-y!* (familiar) / Go ahead!	*Il n'y a pas de quoi.* / You're welcome.
il y a + length of time / ago:	*Y a-t-il . . . ?* / Is there . . . ? Are there . . . ?
il y a un mois / a month ago	
il y a / there is, there are	*y compris* / including
il y avait . . . / there was (there were) . . .	

Examples:
Y a-t-il un stylo dans ton bureau? / Is there a pen in your desk?
Oui, il y en a un. Vas-y. Prends-le. / Yes, there is one. Go ahead. Take it.

§13.

Dates, Days, Months, Seasons

§13.1 Dates

Quelle est la date aujourd'hui? / What's the date today?

C'est aujourd'hui le premier octobre. / Today is October first.
C'est aujourd'hui le deux novembre. / Today is November second.
C'est quel jour aujourd'hui? or *Quel jour sommes-nous aujourd'hui?* / What day is it today?
C'est lundi. / It's Monday.
C'est aujourd'hui mardi. / Today is Tuesday.

Quand êtes-vous né(e)? / When were you born?
Je suis né(e) le vingt-deux août, mil neuf cent soixante-six. / I was born on August 22, 1966.

Use the cardinal numbers for dates, except "the first," which is *le premier*.

§13.2 Days

The days of the week, which are all masculine, are:

lundi / Monday
mardi / Tuesday
mercredi / Wednesday
jeudi / Thursday

vendredi / Friday
samedi / Saturday
dimanche / Sunday

177

To talk about something that happens repeatedly on a certain day of the week, use the definite article:

Le samedi, nous allons au parc. / On Saturdays, we go to the park.

To talk about an upcoming day of the week, you do not need the definite article:

J'ai un examen mardi. / I have a test on Tuesday. (That is, next Tuesday.)

The days of the week are not capitalized in French. However, they are capitalized if they are placed at the beginning of a sentence:

Vendredi, je prends le TGV pour aller à Rennes. / On Friday, I will take the TGV to Rennes. (*le TGV = le train à grande vitesse* / high-speed train)

| Tip | On a French calendar, the week starts on Monday, not Sunday. |

Janvier 2027						
L	M	M	J	V	S	D
				1	2	3
4	5	6	7	8	9	10
11	12	13	14	15	16	17
18	19	20	21	22	23	24
25	26	27	28	29	30	31

§13.3 Months

The months of the year, which are all masculine, are:

janvier / January
février / February
mars / March
avril / April
mai / May
juin / June

juillet / July
août / August
septembre / September
octobre / October
novembre / November
décembre / December

§13

To say "in" + the name of the month, use *en: en janvier, en février*; OR *au mois de janvier, au mois de février* / in the month of January, etc.

As with the days of the week, the months are not capitalized in French, except at the beginning of a sentence (see §2.1).

§13.4 Seasons

The seasons of the year, which are all masculine, are:

le printemps / spring
l'été / summer

l'automne / fall
l'hiver / winter

| Tip | *En hiver*, you shiver. |

To say "in" + the name of the season, use *en* except with *printemps: au printemps, en été, en automne, en hiver* / in spring, in summer, in autumn, in winter.

In French, there are adjectives that are associated with the seasons:

printanier, printanière / spring; *une salade printanière* / garden salad

estival, estivale / summer

automnal, automnale / autumnal

hivernal, hivernale / winter

Example:
Malheureusement, la piste de ski est fermée pendant la saison estivale. / Unfortunately, the ski slope is closed during the summer season.

§14.

Telling Time

§14.1 TIME EXPRESSIONS YOU OUGHT TO KNOW

Quelle heure est-il? / What time is it?
Il est une heure. / It is one o'clock.
Il est une heure dix. / It is ten minutes after one.
Il est une heure et quart. / It is a quarter after one.
Il est deux heures et demie. / It is half past two; it is two thirty.
Il est trois heures moins vingt. / It is twenty minutes to three.
Il est trois heures moins le quart. / It is a quarter to three.
Il est midi. / It is noon.
Il est minuit. / It is midnight.
à quelle heure? / at what time?
à une heure / at one o'clock
à une heure précise / at exactly one o'clock
à deux heures pile / at two o'clock on the dot
à deux heures précises / at exactly two o'clock
à neuf heures du matin / at nine in the morning
à trois heures de l'après-midi / at three in the afternoon
à dix heures du soir / at ten in the evening
à l'heure / on time
à temps / in time
vers trois heures / around three o'clock; about three o'clock
un quart d'heure / a quarter of an hour; a quarter hour
une demi-heure / a half hour
Il est midi et demi / It is twelve thirty; It is half past twelve (noon).
Il est minuit et demi. / It is twelve thirty; It is half past twelve (midnight).

Il est une heure.

Il est deux heures.

Il est deux heures vingt.

Il est cinq heures et quart.

Il est huit heures et demie.

Il est onze heures moins le quart.

Il est onze heures moins dix.

* In telling time, *Il est* + the hour is used, whether it is one or more than one, *e.g., Il est une heure. Il est deux heures.*
* If the time is after the hour, state the hour, then the minutes: *Il est une heure dix.*
* The conjunction *et* is used with *quart* after the hour and with *demi* or *demie: Il est une heure et quart. Il est une heure et demie. Il est midi et demi.*

     The masculine form *demi* is used after a masculine noun: *Il est midi et demi.* The feminine form *demie* is used after a feminine noun: *Il est deux heures et demie.*

     Demi remains *demi* when before a feminine or masculine noun, and is joined to the noun with a hyphen: *une demi-heure.*
* If the time expressed is before the hour, *moins* is used: *Il est trois heures moins vingt.*
* A quarter to the hour is *moins le quart.*
* To express A.M. use *du matin*; to express P.M. use *de l'après-midi* if the time is in the afternoon; *du soir* if in the evening.

§14.2 "OFFICIAL" TIME EXPRESSIONS

Another way to tell time is the official time used by the French government on radio and TV, in railroad and bus stations, and at airports.

- It is the twenty-four-hour system.
- In this system, *quart, demi, demie, moins*, and *et* are not used.
- When you hear or see the stated time, if the number is less than twelve, it is A.M. time, except for *24 heures,* which is midnight; *zéro heure* is also midnight. When the hour is greater than 12 (that is, from 13 through 23), subtract twelve from the number you see or hear.

Examples:

> *Il est dix heures trente.* / It is 10:30 A.M.
> *Il est treize heures.* / It is 1:00 P.M.
> *Il est quinze heures.* / It is 3:00 P.M.
> *Il est vingt heures trente.* / It is 8:30 P.M.
> *Il est minuit.* / It is midnight.
> *Il est seize heures trente.* / It is 4:30 P.M.
> *Il est dix-huit heures quinze.* / It is 6:15 P.M.
> *Il est vingt heures quarante-cinq.* / It is 8:45 P.M.
> *Il est vingt-deux heures cinquante.* / It is 10:50 P.M.

The abbreviation for *heure* or *heures* is *h.*

Examples:

> *Il est 20 h 20.* / It is 8:20 P.M.
> *Il est 15 h 50.* / It is 3:50 P.M.
> *Il est 23 h 30.* / It is 11:30 P.M.

§15.

Talking About the Weather

Quel temps fait-il? / What's the weather like?

WITH *Il fait . . .*

Il fait beau. / The weather is fine. The weather is beautiful.
Il fait beau temps. / The weather is beautiful.
Il fait chaud. / It's warm.
Il fait clair. / It is clear.
Il fait doux. / It's mild.
Il fait du soleil. / It's sunny. (You can also say *Il fait soleil.*)
Il fait du tonnerre. / It's thundering. (OR: *Il tonne.*)
Il fait du vent. / It's windy.
Il fait frais. / It is cool.
Il fait froid. / It's cold.
Il fait humide. / It's humid.
Il fait mauvais. / The weather is bad.

15

WITH *Il fait un temps . . .*

Il fait un temps affreux. / The weather is frightful.
Il fait un temps calme. / The weather is calm.
Il fait un temps couvert. / The weather is cloudy.
Il fait un temps lourd. / It's muggy.
Il fait un temps magnifique. / The weather is magnificent.
Il fait un temps superbe. / The weather is superb.

WITH *Le temps* + VERB . . .

Le temps menace. / The weather is threatening.
Le temps se gâte. / The weather is getting bad.
Le temps se met au beau. / The weather is getting beautiful.
Le temps se met au froid. / It's getting cold.
Le temps se rafraîchit. / The weather is getting cool.

WITH *Le ciel est . . .*

Le ciel est bleu. / The sky is blue.
Le ciel est calme. / The sky is calm.
Le ciel est couvert. / The sky is cloudy.
Le ciel est gris. / The sky is gray.

WITH OTHER VERBS

Il gèle. / It's freezing.
Il grêle. / It's hailing.
Il neige. / It's snowing.
Il pleut. / It's raining.
Il tombe de la grêle. / It's hailing.

La Température / Temperature

When traveling to francophone regions, it helps to be familiar with the metric system. When you see or hear a weather forecast, the temperature will be given in Celsius/Centigrade instead of Fahrenheit.

To ask what the temperature is, you can say:

Quelle est la température? or *Quelle température fait-il?* / What is the temperature?

OR

Il fait combien? / What's the temperature? (In this situation, it is implied that you are talking about the temperature.)

The response may be:

La température est (de) vingt degrés. / It's twenty degrees. (This temperature is in Celsius. See below for a tip on Celsius-Fahrenheit conversion.)

OR

Il fait vingt-cinq. OR *Il fait vingt-cinq degrés.* / It's twenty-five (degrees). (Note: Once again, this is in Celsius.)

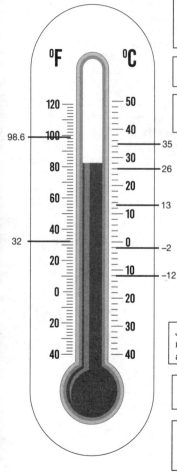

Il fait trente-cinq. / It's thirty-five.
Il fait très chaud! / It's very hot!
Je mets un maillot de bain. /
I put on a swimsuit.

Il fait vingt-six. / It's twenty-six.
Il fait chaud. / It's hot.

Je mets un short et un T-shirt. /
I put on shorts and a T-shirt.

Il fait treize. / It's thirteen
degrees.
Il fait frais. / It's cool.

*Je porte un pantalon et un
pull.* / I wear pants and a
sweater.

Il fait moins deux. / It's two
below.
Il fait froid et il neige. / It's
cold and it's snowing.

*Je mets un manteau d'hiver, un
foulard et des bottes.* / I put on
a winter coat, a scarf, and boots.

Il fait moins douze. / It's twelve
below.

Il fait très froid! / It's very cold!
Je reste chez moi! / I stay at
home!

§15

Conversion from Celsius to Fahrenheit is commonly given as: 9/5 Celsius + 32 = Fahrenheit. However, it's a challenge for most people to multiply by nine and divide by five in your head. Instead, simply double the Celsius temperature, subtract one tenth of that total, and then add 32.

For example:

35°C to Fahrenheit
35°C × 2 = 70
70 − 7 = 63
63 + 32 = 95°F

That's hot!

 If your body temperature goes significantly above 37°C / 98.6°F, you may need to see a doctor:
J'ai de la fièvre. / I have a fever. OR I have a temperature.
J'ai 38 de fièvre. / I have a temperature of 100.4.

§16.

Numbers

Cardinal Numbers: 1 to 1000

0 *zéro*	40 *quarante*
1 *un, une*	41 *quarante et un*
2 *deux*	42 *quarante-deux*, etc.
3 *trois*	
4 *quatre*	50 *cinquante*
5 *cinq*	51 *cinquante et un*
6 *six*	52 *cinquante-deux*, etc.
7 *sept*	
8 *huit*	60 *soixante*
9 *neuf*	61 *soixante et un*
10 *dix*	62 *soixante-deux*, etc.
11 *onze*	
12 *douze*	70 *soixante-dix*
13 *treize*	71 *soixante et onze*
14 *quatorze*	72 *soixante-douze*, etc.
15 *quinze*	
16 *seize*	80 *quatre-vingts*
17 *dix-sept*	81 *quatre-vingt-un*
18 *dix-huit*	82 *quatre-vingt-deux*, etc.
19 *dix-neuf*	
	90 *quatre-vingt-dix*
	91 *quatre-vingt-onze*
20 *vingt*	92 *quatre-vingt-douze*,
21 *vingt et un*	etc.
22 *vingt-deux*, etc.	
	100 *cent*
30 *trente*	101 *cent un*
31 *trente et un*	102 *cent deux*, etc.
32 *trente-deux*, etc.	

200 *deux cents* 201 *deux cent un* 202 *deux cent deux*, etc.	1 000 *mille* 1 001 *mille un* 2 000 *deux mille* 5 000 *cinq mille* 5 150 *cinq mille cent* *cinquante*
300 *trois cents* 301 *trois cent un* 302 *trois cent deux*, etc.	

	20 000 *vingt mille*
	35 000 *trente-cinq mille*
	85 842 *quatre-vingt-cinq*
	    mille huit cent
	    quarante-deux

400 *quatre cents* 401 *quatre cent un* 402 *quatre cent deux*, etc.	
500 *cinq cents* 501 *cinq cent un* 502 *cinq cent deux*, etc.	100 000 *cent mille* 200 000 *deux cent mille* 350 000 *trois cent* *cinquante mille* 800 000 *huit cent mille*
600 *six cents* 601 *six cent un* 602 *six cent deux*, etc.	

700 *sept cents*
701 *sept cent un*
702 *sept cent deux*, etc.
	1 000 000 *un million*
	2 000 000 *deux*
	    millions
	200 000 000 *deux cent*
	    millions

800 *huit cents* 801 *huit cent un* 802 *huit cent deux*, etc.	1 000 000 000 *un milliard* 2 000 000 000 *deux* *milliards*
900 *neuf cents* 901 *neuf cent un* 902 *neuf cent deux*, etc.	

Tip   Pronounce *seize* (16) as in English "**Says** who?"

Simple Arithmetical Expressions

deux et deux font quatre	2 + 2 = 4
trois fois cinq font quinze	3 × 5 = 15
douze moins dix font deux	12 – 10 = 2
dix divisés par deux font cinq	10 ÷ 2 = 5

Fractions

$\frac{1}{2}$	*un demi*	a (one) half
$\frac{1}{3}$	*un tiers*	a (one) third
$\frac{1}{4}$	*un quart*	a (one) fourth
$\frac{1}{5}$	*un cinquième*	a (one) fifth

§16

Approximate Amounts

une dizaine	about ten
une quinzaine	about fifteen
une vingtaine	about twenty
une trentaine	about thirty
une quarantaine	about forty
une cinquantaine	about fifty
une soixantaine	about sixty
une centaine	about a hundred
un millier	about a thousand

Tip You can remember that *une quarantaine* is about 40 because there are 40 days in a "quarantine."

Ordinal Numbers: First to Fiftieth

first	*premier, première*	1st	1er, 1re
second	*deuxième (second, seconde)*	2nd	2^e
third	*troisième*	3rd	3^e
fourth	*quatrième*	4th	4^e
fifth	*cinquième*	5th	5^e
sixth	*sixième*	6th	6^e
seventh	*septième*	7th	7^e
eighth	*huitième*	8th	8^e
ninth	*neuvième*	9th	9^e
tenth	*dixième*	10th	10^e
eleventh	*onzième*	11th	11^e
twelfth	*douzième*	12th	12^e
thirteenth	*treizième*	13th	13^e
fourteenth	*quatorzième*	14th	14^e
fifteenth	*quinzième*	15th	15^e
sixteenth	*seizième*	16th	16^e
seventeenth	*dix-septième*	17th	17^e
eighteenth	*dix-huitième*	18th	18^e
nineteenth	*dix-neuvième*	19th	19^e
twentieth	*vingtième*	20th	20^e
twenty-first	*vingt et unième*	21st	21^e
twenty-second	*vingt-deuxième*	22nd	22^e
twenty-third	*vingt-troisième*	23rd	23^e
twenty-fourth	*vingt-quatrième*	24th	24^e
twenty-fifth	*vingt-cinquième*	25th	25^e
twenty-sixth	*vingt-sixième*	26th	26^e
twenty-seventh	*vingt-septième*	27th	27^e
twenty-eighth	*vingt-huitième*	28th	28^e
twenty-ninth	*vingt-neuvième*	29th	29^e
thirtieth	*trentième*	30th	30^e
fortieth	*quarantième*	40th	40^e
fiftieth	*cinquantième*	50th	50^e
and so on.			

Notice that an ordinal number is generally formed by adding the suffix *-ième* to the cardinal number. Before adding the suffix, we must drop the final mute *e* of a cardinal number, if there is one, as in *treize/treizième; trente/trentième*. If you have difficulty forming the ordinal numbers after 50th, you can usually find them in a standard English-French dictionary.

Some observations:

- You must learn the difference between cardinal and ordinal numbers. If you have trouble distinguishing between the two, just remember that we use cardinal numbers most of the time: *un, deux, trois* (one, two, three), and so on.
- Use ordinal numbers to express a certain order: *premier (première*, if the noun following is feminine), *deuxième, troisième* (first, second, third), and so on.
- *Premier* is the masculine singular form and *première* is the feminine singular form. Examples: *le premier homme* / the first man, *la première femme* / the first woman.
- The masculine singular form *second*, or the feminine singular form *seconde*, is used to mean "second" when there are only two. When there are more than two, *deuxième* is used: *le Second Empire*, because there were only two empires in France, but *la Deuxième République*, because there have been more than two republics in France.
- The raised letters in *1er* are the last two letters in the word *premier*; it is equivalent to our "st" in 1st. The raised letters in *1re* are the last two letters in the word *première*, which is the feminine singular form of "first."

§16

The raised letter *e* after an ordinal number (for example, 2e) stands for the *-ième* ending of a French ordinal number.

- When referring to sovereigns or rulers, the only ordinal number used is *premier*. For all other designations, the cardinal numbers are used. The definite article "the" is used in English but not in French. Examples:

François 1er	*François Premier*	Francis the First
	BUT	
Louis XIV	*Louis Quatorze*	Louis the Fourteenth

§17.

Synonyms

Synonyms are words with the same or nearly the same meaning.

aide n.f., *secours* n.m.	aid, help
aimer mieux v., *préférer*	to like better, prefer
aliment n.m., *nourriture* n.f.	food, nourishment
anneau n.m., *bague* n.f.	ring (on finger)
arriver v., *se passer*	to happen, occur
aussitôt que conj., *dès que*	as soon as
auteur n.m., *auteure* n.f.; *écrivain* n.m., *écrivaine* n.f.	author, writer
bâtiment n.m., *édifice* n.m.	building, edifice
bâtir v., *construire*	to build, construct
beaucoup de adv., *bien des*	many
bref. brève adj., *court, courte*	brief, short
casser v., *rompre, briser*	to break
causer v., *parler*	to chat, talk
centre n.m., *milieu* n.m.	center, middle
certain (certaine) adj., *sûr, sûre*	certain, sure
cesser v., *arrêter*	to cease, to stop
chagrin n.m., *souci* n.m.	sorrow, trouble, care, concern
chemin n.m., *route* n.f.	road, route
commencer à + infinitive, v., *se mettre à* + infinitive	to commence, begin, start
conseil n.m., *avis* n.m.	counsel, advice, opinion

adj.: adjective; adv.: adverb; conj.: conjunction; f.: feminine;
m.: masculine; n.: noun; prep.: preposition; v.: verb

content, (contente) adj., *heureux (heureuse)*	content, happy
de façon que conj., *de manière que*	so that, in such a way
décéder v., *mourir*	to die
dégoût n.m., *répugnance* n.f.	disgust, repugnance
dérober v., *voler*	to rob, steal
désirer v., *vouloir*	to desire, want
disputer v., *contester*	to dispute, argue, contest
docteur n.m., *médecin* n.m.	doctor, physician
embrasser v., *donner un baiser*	to embrace, hug; to give a kiss
employer v., *se servir de*	to employ, use, make use of
épouvanter v., *effrayer*	to frighten, terrify, scare
erreur n.f., *faute* n.f.	error, fault, mistake
espèce n.f., *sorte* n.f.	species, type, kind, sort
essayer de + infinitive, v., *tâcher de* + infinitive	to try, to attempt + infinitive
façon n.f., *manière* n.f.	way, manner
fameux, (fameuse) adj., *célèbre*	famous, celebrated
fatigué, (fatiguée) adj., *épuisé, (épuisée)*	tired, fatigued, exhausted
favori, (favorite) adj., *préféré (préférée)*	favorite, preferred
fin n.f., *bout* n.m.	end
finir v., *terminer*	to finish, end, terminate
frémir v., *trembler*	to shiver, quiver, tremble
gaspiller v., *dissiper*	to waste, dissipate
gâter v., *abîmer*	to spoil, ruin, damage
glace n.f., *miroir* n.m.	hand mirror, mirror
grossier, grossière adj., *vulgaire*	gross, vulgar, cheap, common

habiter v., *demeurer*	to live (in), dwell, inhabit
haïr v., *détester*	to hate, detest
indiquer v., *montrer*	to indicate, show
jadis adv., *autrefois*	formerly, in times gone by
jeu n.m., *divertissement* n.m.	game, amusement
labourer v., *travailler*	to labor, work
laisser v., *permettre*	to allow, permit
lier v., *attacher*	to tie, attach
lieu n.m., *endroit* n.m.	place, spot, location
logis n.m. *habitation* n.f.	lodging, dwelling
lutter v., *combattre*	to struggle, fight, combat
maître n.m. *instituteur* n.m.	master, teacher, instructor
maîtresse n.f. *institutrice* n.f.	mistress, teacher, instructor
mauvais (mauvaise) adj., *méchant (méchante)*	bad, mean, nasty
mener v., *conduire*	to lead; to take (someone)
mince adj., *grêle*	thin, slender, skinny
naïf (naïve) adj., *ingénu (ingénue)*	naive, simple, innocent
net (nette) adj., *propre*	neat, clean
noces n.f., *mariage* n.m.	wedding, marriage
obscur adj., *vague*	dark, obscure, vague
œuvre n.f., *travail* n.m.	work
ombrelle n.f., *parasol* n.m.	sunshade, parasol, beach umbrella
parce que conj., *car*	because, for
pareil (pareille) adj., *égal (égale)*	similar, equivalent, equal
parvenir à v., *réussir à*	to succeed, to attain
pays n.m., *nation* n.f.	country, nation
peinture n.f., *tableau* n.m.	painting, picture
pensée n.f., *idée* n.f.	thought, idea
penser v., *réfléchir*	to think, reflect

§17

penser à v., *songer à*	to think of; to dream of
professeur n.m., *maître*, n.m., *maîtresse* n.f.	professor, teacher
puis adv., *ensuite*	then, afterwards
quand conj., *lorsque*	when
quelquefois adv., *parfois*	sometimes, at times
rester v., *demeurer*	to stay, to remain
se rappeler v., *se souvenir de*	to recall, to remember
sérieux (sérieuse) adj., *grave*	serious, grave
seulement adv., *ne* + verb + *que*	only
soin n.m., *attention* n.f.	care, attention
soulier n.m., *chaussure* n.f.	shoe, footwear
tout de suite adv., *immédiatement*	right away, immediately
triste adj., *malheureux (malheureuse)*	sad, unhappy
vêtements n.m., *habits* n.m.	clothes, clothing
visage n.m, *figure* n.f.	face
vite adv., *rapidement*	quickly, rapidly

 Bref (brève, f.) is brief and *court (courte,* f.) is short because it contains the English word "curt" (brief, short).

 Une chaussure is a shoe because it contains *sur* / on, and you put it on your foot.

 Une chaussette is a sock because it's something like an anklet(te) sock.

Tip *Une parole* is a spoken word because when a prisoner is on "*parole*" they give their word that they will behave in a civil manner.

Tip When you give someone *conseil*, you give them counsel, advice.

Tip When you *embrasser* a person, you put your *bras* / arms around that person.

§17

§18.

Antonyms

Antonyms are words with opposite meanings.

absent (absente) adj, absent	*présent (présente)* adj., present
acheter v., to buy	*vendre* v., to sell
agréable adj., pleasant, agreeable	*désagréable* adj., unpleasant, disagreeable
aimable adj., kind	*méchant (méchante)* adj., mean, nasty
aller v., to go	*venir* v., to come
ami (amie) n., friend	*ennemi (ennemie)* n., enemy
s'amuser refl. v., to enjoy oneself, to have a good time	*s'ennuyer* refl. v., to be bored
ancien (ancienne) adj., old, ancient	*nouveau (nouvel, nouvelle)* adj., new
avant prep., before	*après* prep., after
bas (basse) adj., low	*haut (haute)* adj., high
beau (bel, belle) adj., beautiful, handsome	*laid (laide)* adj., ugly
beaucoup (de) adv., much, many	*peu (de)* adv., little, some
beauté n.f., beauty	*laideur* n.f., ugliness
bête adj., stupid	*intelligent (intelligente)* adj., intelligent
bon (bonne) adj., good	*mauvais (mauvaise)* adj., bad
bonheur n.m., happiness	*malheur* n.m., unhappiness

adj.: adjective; adv.: adverb; conj.: conjunction; f.: feminine;
m.: masculine; n.: noun; prep.: preposition v.: verb

chaud (chaude) adj., hot, warm

froid (froide) adj., cold

cher (chère) adj., expensive

bon marché cheap

content (contente) adj., glad, pleased

mécontent (mécontente) adj., displeased

court (courte) adj., short

long (longue) adj., long

debout adv., standing

assis (assise) adj., seated, sitting

dedans adv., inside

dehors adv., outside

demander v., to ask

répondre v., to reply

dernier (dernière) adj., last

premier (première) adj., first

derrière adv., prep., behind, in back of

devant adv., prep., in front of

dessous adv., prep., below, underneath

dessus adv., prep., above, over

différent (différente) adj., different

pareil (pareille) adj., same, similar

difficile adj., difficult

facile adj., easy

domestique adj., domestic

sauvage adj., wild

donner v., to give

recevoir v., to receive

droite n.f., right

gauche n.f., left

emprunter v., to borrow

prêter v., to lend

entrer (dans) v., to enter (in, into)

sortir (de) v., to go out (of, from)

est n.m., east

ouest n.m., west

étroit (étroite) adj., narrow

large adj., wide

faible adj., weak

fort (forte) adj., strong

fermer v., to close

ouvrir v., to open

fin n.f., end

commencement n.m., beginning; *début* n.m., start

finir v., to finish

commencer v., to begin; *se mettre à* v., to begin + inf.

gagner v., to win	*perdre* v., to lose
gai (gaie) adj., gay, happy	*triste* adj., sad
grand (grande) adj., large, tall, big	*petit (petite)* adj., small, little
gros (grosse) adj., fat	*maigre* adj., thin; *mince* adj., thin
grossier (grossière) adj., coarse, impolite	*poli (polie)* adj., polite
heureux (heureuse) adj., happy	*malheureux (malheureuse)* adj., unhappy
ici adv., here	*là-bas* adv., there
inutile adj., useless	*utile* adj., useful
jamais adv., never	*toujours* adv., always
jeune adj., young	*vieux (vieil, vieille)* adj., old
jeunesse n.f., youth	*vieillesse* n.f., old age
joli (jolie) adj., pretty	*laid (laide)* adj., ugly
jour n.m., day	*nuit* n.f., night
léger (légère) adj., light	*lourd (lourde)* adj., heavy
lentement adv., slowly	*vite* adv., quickly
mal adv., badly	*bien* adv., well
moderne adj., modern	*ancien (ancienne)* adj., ancient, old
moins adv., less	*plus* adv., more
monter v., to go up	*descendre* v., to go down
mourir v., to die	*naître* v., to be born
né (née) adj., past part, born	*mort (morte)* adj., past part. died, dead
nord n.m., north	*sud* n.m., south
nouveau (nouvel, nouvelle) adj., new	*vieux (vieil, vieille)* adj., old
obéir (à) v., to obey	*désobéir (à)* v., to disobey
ôter v., to remove, to take off	*mettre* v., to put, to put on

§18

oui adv., yes	*non* adv., no
paix n.f., peace	*guerre* n.f., war
paraître v., to appear	*disparaître* v., to disappear
paresseux (paresseuse) adj., lazy	*travailleur (travailleuse)* adj., diligent
partir v., to leave	*arriver* v., to arrive
pauvre adj., poor	*riche* adj., rich
perdre v., to lose	*trouver* v., to find
plancher n.m., floor	*plafond* n.m., ceiling
plein (pleine) adj., full	*vide* adj., empty
poli (polie) adj., polite	*impoli (impolie)* adj., impolite
possible adj., possible	*impossible* adj., impossible
prendre v., to take	*donner* v. to give
près (de) adv., prep., near	*loin (de)* adv., prep., far (from)
propre adj., clean	*sale* adj., dirty
quelque chose pron., something	*rien* pron., nothing
quelqu'un pron., someone, somebody	*personne* pron., nobody, no one
question n.f., question	*réponse* n.f., answer, reply, response
refuser v., to refuse	*accepter* v., to accept
réussir (à) v., to succeed (at, in)	*échouer (à)* v., to fail (at, in)
rire v., to laugh	*pleurer* v., to cry, to weep
sans prep., without	*avec* prep., with
silence n.m., silence	*bruit* n.m., noise
souvent adv., often	*rarement* adv., rarely
sur prep., on	*sous* prep., under
sûr (sûre) adj., sure, certain	*incertain (incertaine)* adj., unsure, uncertain
tôt adv., early	*tard* adv., late
travailler v., to work	*jouer* v., to play

travailleur (travailleuse) adj., diligent, hardworking	paresseux (paresseuse) adj., lazy
vie n.f., life	mort n.f., death
vivre v., to live	mourir v., to die
vrai (vraie) adj., true	faux (fausse) adj., false

Tip
The verb *mourir* (to die) has one *r* because a person dies once; *nourrir* (to nourish) has two *r*'s because a person is nourished more than once.

Tip
The word *dessous* (below, underneath) contains *sous* (under).

Tip
The word *dessus* (above, over) contains *sus*, which reminds you of *sur* (on).

Tip
Perdre means "to lose" because perdition is a place for lost souls.

Tip
Detroit, a city in Michigan, is on the Detroit River, which is narrow (*étroit*) in spots.

Tip
A floor *(le plancher)* was originally made of wooden planks.

Tip
Pronounce *bonne* as in the English word "bun."

Tip
You "mount" a mountain when you *monter une montagne*.

§18

You go **a**way when you *pa rtir* and you go **o**ut when you *so rtir*. *Partir* and "away" contain **a**'s. *Sortir* and "go out" contain **o**'s.

 If you don't know your right from your left, *droite* contains "it" and so does "right."

§19.

Cognates

In addition to studying synonyms in §17. and antonyms in §18., another good way to increase your vocabulary is to become aware of cognates. A *cognate* is a word whose origin is the same as another word in another language. There are many cognates in French and English whose spelling is sometimes identical or very similar. Most of the time, the meaning is the same or similar; sometimes they appear to be related because of similar spelling, but they are not true cognates. You will find a list of these "false cognates" or "tricky words" in §20.

Generally speaking, certain endings, or suffixes, of French words have English equivalents.

Examples:

French Suffix	Equivalent English Suffix	French Word	English Word
-able	-able	*adorable* / *aimable*	adorable / amiable (likeable)
-aire	-ary	*le dictionnaire*	dictionary
-eux / -euse	-ous	*fameux* / *fameuse*	famous
-ieux / -ieuse	-ous	*gracieux* / *gracieuse*	gracious
-iste	-ist	*le (la) dentiste*	dentist
-ité	-ity	*la qualité*	quality
-ment	-ly	*correctement*	correctly
-mettre	-mit	*admettre*	admit
-oire	-ory	*la mémoire*	memory
-phie	-phy	*la photographie*	photography
-scrire	-scribe	*transcrire*	transcribe

19

A French word that contains the circumflex accent (^) over a vowel means that there used to be an *s* right after that vowel.

Examples:

hâte / haste	*hôtel* / hostel
pâte / paste	*honnête* / honest
bâtard / bastard	*plâtre* / plaster
bête / beast	*île* / isle
fête / feast	*vêpres* / vespers
mât / mast	*prêtre* / priest
château / castle	

But you don't always get a cognate if you insert an *s* right after the vowel that contains a circumflex.

Examples:

gâteau / cake	*bêler* / to bleat
bâtiment / building	*âme* / soul

Tip

If you confuse *le gâteau* (cake) with *le bateau* (boat) because you can't remember which one contains the circumflex accent, remember that the ^ in *gâteau* is the icing on top of the cake!

§20.

Tricky Words

"False friends" ("**faux amis**"/*foh-zamee*) are look-alikes but have different meanings.

There are French words that look like English words but they do not have the same or even similar meaning at all. You must know the following French words and their real meanings. How many others can you think of? Share them with your friends who are studying French. It's a fun way to help build your French vocabulary.

actualités n.f., pl. news reports

actuel adj. present, present-day

actuellement adv. at present

addition n.f. bill (check)

assister v. to attend

attendre v. to wait (for)

belle adj., fem. beautiful

bénir v. to bless

bibliothèque n.f. library (Say *une bibliothèque* when you mean "a library" and *une librairie* when you want to say "a bookstore.")

blesser v. to wound (*Blesser* does not mean "to bless." See *bénir* above.)

cabinet n.m. office; study

car conj. because

causer v. to chat; to cause

cave n.f. cellar, basement

chair n.f. flesh

chargé adj. burdened, loaded

chat n.m. cat

chose n.f. thing

coin n.m. corner

comment adv. how

conférence n.f. lecture

crâne n.m. skull

crayon n.m. pencil

crier v. to shout, cry out

dent n.f. tooth

éditeur n.m. publisher

essence n.f. gasoline

éventuel, éventuelle adj. possible

éventuellement adv. possibly

fin n.f. end
flèche n.f. arrow
fort adj., n. strong
front n.m. forehead

grand adj., m. tall, big, large
grave adj. serious

haïr v. to hate

ignorer v. to be unaware of

journal n.m. newspaper
journée n.f. all day long

large adj. wide, broad
lecture n.f. reading
librairie n.f. bookstore (Say *une librairie* when you want to say "a bookstore" and *une bibliothèque* when you mean "a library.")

magasin n.m. store
main n.f. hand
marine n.f. navy; seascape
médecin n.m. doctor, physician
médecine n.f. medicine (study of)
médicament n.m. medicine
mine n.f. facial appearance
monnaie n.f. change (coins)

occasion n.f. opportunity

pain n.m. bread
par prep. by
personnel adj. personal
pie n.f. magpie (bird)

pile n.f. battery; pile, heap
place n.f. plaza, place
plate adj., fem. flat
pour prep. for
prune n.f. plum
pruneau n.m. prune

quitter v. to leave

raisin n.m. grape
raisin sec n.m. raisin
râpe n.f. grater (cheese)
regarder v. to look (at)
rester v. to remain
roman n.m. novel
rose adj. pink
rose n.f. rose
rue n.f. street

sable n.m. sand
sac n.m. bag, purse
sale adj. dirty, soiled
sensible adj. sensitive
stage n.m. training course of study
stylo n.m. pen

travail n.m. work; *travailler* v. to work (In English, a travail is very difficult or painful work. If you want to say "to travel," the correct translation is *voyager*.)

user v. to wear out

vent n.m. wind (air)
vie n.f. life
voyager v. to travel

§21.

How to Ask a Question

• To ask a question, put **est-ce que** in front of the subject.

> **Est-ce que** vous parlez français?　Do you speak French?
> À quelle heure **est-ce que** le　At what time does the
> train part?　train leave?

• If the first letter of the subject is a vowel or silent *h*, drop **e** in **que** and add an apostrophe.

> **Est-ce qu'**il joue?　Is he playing?
> **Est-ce qu'**Hélène est jolie?　Is Helen pretty?

• If your question is in the negative, put **ne** in front of the verb and **pas** after it.

> **Est-ce que** tu **ne** travailles **pas**?　Aren't you working?
> **Est-ce que** vous **n'**avez **pas**　Don't you have
> d'argent?　any money?

• Instead of using **est-ce que**, you may use the inverted form. Move the subject pronoun and put it after the verb, joining it with a hyphen.

> Parlez-vous français?　Do you speak French?
> **Ne** parlez-vous **pas** anglais?　Don't you speak
> 　English?

21

• If the subject pronoun is **je**, do not use the inverted form. Use **est-ce que**. The inverted form with **je** is used only with certain verbs, for example:

Que sais-je?	What do I know?
Où suis-je?	Where am I?
Ai-je assez d'argent?	Do I have enough money?

Puis-je aller aux toilettes? / May I go to the restroom? (The first person present tense of *pouvoir* / to be able can be either *je peux* or *je puis*.)

• In the inverted form, if the last letter of the verb is a vowel in the third person singular, insert **-t-** between the verb and the subject pronouns **il**, **elle**, or **on**.

Danse-**t**-il?	Does he dance? Is he dancing?
À quelle heure arrive-**t**-elle?	At what time is she arriving?
Où va-**t**-on?	Where is one going?

• In the inverted form, if the subject is a noun, mention the noun first and use the pronoun of the noun.

Le docteur va-**t**-il venir bientôt?	Is the doctor going to come soon?

• To ask a question with *il y a*, you can use *est-ce que*.

Est-ce qu'il y a un guichet automatique près d'ici? / Is there an ATM near here?

• You can also invert *il y a*: *Y a-t-il . . .* / Is there?

Y a-t-il une pharmacie dans le quartier? / Is there a pharmacy in the neighborhood?

§22.

Definitions of Basic Grammatical Terms with Examples in French and English Beginner, Intermediate, and Advanced Levels

Active voice

When we speak or write in the active voice, the subject of the verb performs the action. The action falls on the direct object.

> **Example:**
> Everyone loves Janine. / *Tout le monde aime Janine.*
> The subject is **everyone** / *tout le monde*. The verb is **loves** / *aime*.
>   The direct object is **Janine**.

See also **passive voice** in this section and in §7.9.

Adjective

An adjective is a word that modifies a noun or a pronoun. In grammar, to modify a word means to describe, limit, expand, or make the meaning particular. In French, an adjective agrees in gender (masculine or feminine) and in number (singular or plural) with the noun or pronoun it modifies.

> **Examples:**
> This garden is beautiful. / *Ce jardin est beau.*
> She is beautiful. / *Elle est belle.*
> The adjective **beautiful** / *beau* modifies the noun **garden** / *jardin*. It
>   is masculine singular because *le jardin* is masculine singular.

The adjective **beautiful** / *belle* modifies the pronoun **She** / *Elle*. It is feminine singular because **she** is feminine singular.

When an adjective modifies a noun (or people) of mixed gender, the masculine plural is used, even if there is only one masculine noun or person:

Marie, Suzanne et Sandra sont *grandes*. / Mary, Suzanne, and Sandra are tall. (Fem. pl.)

Robert, Marie, Suzanne et Sandra sont *grands*. / Robert, Mary, Suzanne, and Sandra are tall. (Masc. pl.)

Review *être* in the verb tables in §7.19. In French, there are different kinds of adjectives. See also **comparative adjective**, **demonstrative adjective**, **descriptive adjective**, **interrogative adjective**, **limiting adjective**, **possessive adjective**, and **superlative adjective** in this section.

Adverb

An adverb is a word that modifies a verb, an adjective, or another adverb. An adverb says something about how, when, where, to what extent, or in what way.

Examples:

Jane runs swiftly. / *Jeanne court rapidement.* The adverb **swiftly** / *rapidement* modifies the verb **runs** / *court*. The adverb shows *how* she runs.

Jack is a very good friend. / *Jacques est un très bon ami.* The adverb **very** / très modifies the adjective **good** / *bon*. The adverb shows *how good* a friend he is.

The boy is eating too fast now. / *Le garçon mange trop vite maintenant.* The adverb **too** / *trop* modifies the adverb **fast** / *vite*. The adverb shows to what extent he is eating fast. The adverb **now** / *maintenant* tells us when.

The post office is there. / *Le bureau de poste est là.* The adverb **there** / *là* modifies the verb **is** / *est.* It tells us where the post office is.

Mary writes carefully. / *Marie écrit soigneusement.* The adverb **carefully** / *soigneusement* modifies the verb **writes** / *écrit.* It tells us in what way she writes.

Affirmative statement, negative statement

A statement in the affirmative is the opposite of a statement in the negative. To negate an affirmative statement is to make it negative.

> **Examples:**
> In the affirmative: I like chocolate ice cream. / *J'aime la glace au chocolat*.
> In the negative: I do not like chocolate ice cream. / *Je n'aime pas la glace au chocolat*.

Note that the helping verb is negated in the *passé composé*.
> *Madeleine a donné la pomme à son cheval.* / Madeleine gave the apple to her horse.
> *Madeleine n'a pas donné la pomme à son cheval.* / Madeleine did not give the apple to her horse.

Agreement of adjective with noun

An adjective agrees in both gender (masculine or feminine) and number (singular or plural) with the noun that it modifies.

> **Examples:**
> **a white house** / *une maison blanche.* The adjective *blanche* is feminine singular because the noun *une maison* is feminine singular.
> **two white houses** / *deux maisons blanches.* The adjective *blanches* is feminine plural because the noun *maisons* is feminine plural.

When the nouns are of mixed gender (masculine or feminine), a masculine plural adjective is used, even if only one of the nouns is masculine in gender:
> Il portait une chemise et un pantalon *bleus.* / He was wearing a blue shirt and blue pants.

Agreement of past participle of a reflexive verb with its reflexive pronoun

When a reflexive pronoun is the **direct object** of a reflexive verb, the past participle agrees with it in both gender (masculine

§22

or feminine) and number (singular or plural). The agreement is determined by looking at the subject to see its gender and number, which is the same as its reflexive pronoun. If the reflexive pronoun is the **indirect object**, an agreement is not made.

Examples:

to wash oneself / *se laver*

She washed herself. / *Elle s'est lavée*. There is a feminine agreement on the past participle *lavée* (added *e*) with the reflexive pronoun *se* (here, *s'*) because it serves as a direct object pronoun. What or whom did she wash? Herself, which is expressed in *se (s')*.

BUT:

She washed her hair. / *Elle s'est lavé les cheveux*. There is no feminine agreement on the past participle *lavé* here because the reflexive pronoun *(se,* here, *s')* serves as an **indirect object**. The direct object is *les cheveux,* and it is stated after the verb. What did she wash? She washed her hair **on herself** *(s')*.

Always be aware of where the action of the verb is carried out. Is there a preposition?

Mon père a téléphoné à ma mère. / My father called (phoned) my mother.

Ils se sont téléphoné. / They called (phoned) each other. (There is no agreement on *téléphoné* because se is not a preceding direct object pronoun. It is an indirect object because the expression is *téléphoner à.*)

Similarly, you would say: *Anne s'est préparée pour le concours.* / Anne prepared herself for the contest.

But: *Anne s'est préparé un sandwich.* / Anne prepared (made) herself a sandwich. In this sentence, *se (s')* is not a direct object. What did she prepare (make)? A sandwich <u>for</u> herself *(se)*.

See **reflexive verbs** in the Index. See also **reflexive pronoun** and **reflexive verb** in this section.

Agreement of past participle with its preceding direct object

When a verb is conjugated with *avoir* in the compound tenses, agreement is made on the past participle with the direct object in both gender (masculine or feminine) and number (singular or plural). Agreement is made when the direct object, if there is one, *precedes* the verb.

Examples:

Where are the cookies? Paul ate them. / *Où sont les biscuits? Paul les a mangés.* The verb *a mangés* is in the *passé composé; a manger* is conjugated with *avoir.* There is a plural agreement on the past participle *mangés* (added s) because the preceding direct object **them** / *les* is masculine plural, referring to *les biscuits,* which is masculine plural.

Who wrote the letters? Robert wrote them. / *Qui a écrit les lettres? Robert les a écrites.* The verb *a écrites* is in the passé composé; *écrire* is conjugated with *avoir.* There is a feminine plural agreement on the past participle *écrites* (added e and s) because the preceding direct object **them** / *les* is feminine plural, referring to *les lettres,* which is feminine plural. A past participle functions as an adjective. An agreement in gender and number is not made with an indirect object: Robert talked to them. / *Robert leur a parlé. Leur* is an indirect object (to them).

Review the *passé composé.* See also **direct object noun** and **direct object pronoun** in this list.

Agreement of past participle with the subject

When a verb is conjugated with *être* in the compound tenses, agreement is made on the past participle with the subject in both gender (masculine or feminine) and number (singular or plural).

Examples:

She went to Montreal. / *Elle est allée à Montréal.* The verb *est allée* is in the *passé composé; aller* is conjugated with *être.* There is a feminine agreement on the past participle *allée* (added e) because the subject *elle* is feminine singular.

The boys have arrived. / *Les garçons sont arrivés.* The verb *sont arrivés* is in the *passé composé; arriver* is conjugated with *être.* There is a plural agreement on the past participle *arrivés* (added *s*) because the subject *les garçons* is masculine plural. Review verbs conjugated with *avoir* or *être* to form the *passé composé* tense in §7.3–1. See also **past participle** and **subject** in this section.

Agreement of verb with its subject

A verb agrees in person (1st, 2nd, or 3rd) and in number (singular or plural) with its subject.

Examples:
Does he always tell the truth? / *Dit-il toujours la vérité?* The verb *dit* (of *dire*) is third person singular because the subject *il* / **he** is third person singular.

Where are they going? / *Où vont-ils?* The verb *vont* (of *aller*) is third person plural because the subject *ils* / **they** is third person plural. Review *aller* in the verb tables in §7.19. For subject pronouns in the singular and plural, see §6.1–1.

Antecedent

An antecedent is a word to which a relative pronoun refers. It comes before the pronoun.

Examples:
The girl who is laughing over there is my sister. / *La jeune fille qui rit là-bas est ma soeur.* The antecedent is **girl** / *la jeune fille.* The relative pronoun **who** / *qui* refers to the girl.

The car that I bought is expensive. / *La voiture que j'ai achetée est chère.* The antecedent is **car** / *la voiture.* The relative pronoun **that** / *que* refers to the car. Note also that the past participle *achetée* is feminine singular because it refers to *la voiture* (fem. sing.), which precedes the verb. See also **relative pronoun** in this section.

Auxiliary verb

An auxiliary verb is a helping verb. In English grammar, it is
to have. In French grammar, it is *avoir* (to have) or *être* (to be).
An auxiliary verb is used to help form the *passé composé*
tense and the other compound tenses.

Examples:
I have eaten. (I ate. I did eat.) / *J'ai mangé.*
She has left. (She left. She did leave.) / *Elle est partie.*
Review verbs conjugated with either *avoir* or *être* as helping verbs
to form the *passé composé* in §7.3–1.

Cardinal number

A cardinal number is a number that expresses an amount,
such as one, two, three, and so on.

See also **ordinal number** in this section.

Tip	Cardinal numbers are used for counting. "How many cardinals did you count on the fence?" "I counted seven cardinals."

Causative *faire*

In English grammar, a causative verb causes something to be
done. In French grammar, the idea is the same. The subject of
the verb causes the action expressed in the verb to be carried
out by someone else.

Example:
Mr. Reisner is having a house built. / *Monsieur Reisner fait
construire une maison.*
Review *faire* in the verb tables in §7.19.

Clause

A clause is a group of words that contains a subject and a predicate. A predicate may contain more than one word. A conjugated verb form is revealed in the predicate.

> **Example:**
> Mrs. Coty lives in a small apartment. / *Madame Coty demeure dans un petit appartement.*
> The subject is **Mrs. Coty** / *Madame Coty.* The predicate is **lives in a small apartment** / *demeure dans un petit appartement.* The verb is **lives** / *demeure.*

See also **dependent clause, independent clause,** and **predicate** in this section.

Comparative adjective

When making a comparison between two persons or things, an adjective is used to express the degree of comparison in the following ways.

Of the same degree of comparison:
> Raymond is **as tall as** his father. / *Raymond est **aussi grand que** son père.*

Of a lesser degree of comparison:
> Monique is **less intelligent than** her sister. / *Monique est **moins intelligente que** sa soeur.*

Of a higher degree of comparison:
> This apple is **more delicious than** that apple. / *Cette pomme-ci est **plus délicieuse que** cette pomme-là.*

See **comparative adjectives** and **superlative adjectives** in §5.4–5.

Comparative adverb

An adverb is compared in the same way as an adjective is compared. See **comparative adjective** (above).

Of the same degree of comparison:
> Mr. Bernard speaks **as fast as** Mr. Claude. / *Monsieur Bernard parle **aussi vite que** Monsieur Claude.*

Of a lesser degree of comparison:
> Alice studies **less seriously than** her sister. / *Alice étudie **moins sérieusement que** sa soeur.*

Of a higher degree of comparison:
> Albert works **more slowly than** his brother. / *Albert travaille **plus lentement que** son frère.*

Review **comparative adverbs** and **superlative adverbs** in §8.3–3. See also **superlative adverb** in this section.

Complex sentence

A complex sentence contains one independent clause and one or more dependent clauses.

> **Examples:**

One independent clause and one dependent clause:
> Jack is handsome but his brother isn't. / *Jacques est beau mais son frère ne l'est pas.* The independent clause is **Jack is handsome.** It makes sense when it stands alone because it expresses a complete thought. The dependent clause is **but his brother isn't.** The dependent clause, which is introduced by the conjunction **but,** does not make complete sense when it stands alone because it depends on the thought expressed in the independent clause.

One independent clause and two dependent clauses:
> Mary likes winter because she loves downhill skiing, but she hates the cold. / *Marie aime l'hiver parce qu'elle adore le ski alpin, mais elle déteste le froid*. The independent clause is **Mary likes winter.** It makes sense when it stands alone because it expresses a complete thought. The first dependent clause is **because she loves downhill skiing.** This dependent clause, which is introduced by the conjunction **because**, does not make complete sense when it stands alone because it depends on the thought expressed in the independent clause.

§22

The second dependent clause is **but she hates the cold.** That dependent clause, which is introduced by the conjunction **but,** does not make complete sense either when it stands alone because it depends on the thought expressed in the independent clause. See also **dependent clause** and **independent clause** in this section.

Compound sentence

A compound sentence contains two or more independent clauses.

Example:
Mrs. Dubois went to the supermarket, bought some groceries, and then returned home. / *Madame Dubois est allée au supermarché, elle a acheté des provisions, et puis elle est rentrée chez elle.* This compound sentence contains three independent clauses. They are independent because they make sense when they stand alone. Review the *passé composé* in the Index. See also **clause** and **independent clause** in this section.

Conjugation

The conjugation of a verb is the fixed order of all its forms showing their inflections (changes) in the three persons of the singular and the three persons of the plural in a particular tense.

In French, there are three major types of regular verb conjugations:
    1st conjugation type: regular verbs that end in *er;* for example, *donner.*
    2nd conjugation type: regular verbs that end in *ir;* for example, *finir.*
    3rd conjugation type: regular verbs that end in *re;* for example, *vendre.*

Verbs that end in *-oir (avoir, devoir, pouvoir, vouloir,* and others) can be considered a separate group. However, they are irregular and need to be learned individually.

Conjunction

A conjunction is a word that connects words or groups of words.

> **Examples:**
> **and** / *et*, **or** / *ou*, **but** / *mais*
> You **and** I are going downtown. / *Toi **et** moi, nous allons en ville.*
> You can stay home **or** you can come with us. / *Tu peux rester à la maison **ou** tu peux venir avec nous.*

Declarative sentence

A declarative sentence makes a statement.

> **Example:**
> I have finished the work. / *J'ai fini le travail.*

Review the *passé composé* in §7.8–8. See also **interrogative sentence** in this section.

Definite article

The definite article in French has four forms, and they all mean **the**.
They are: *le, la, l', les*, as in:

> *le livre* / **the book**, *la maison* / **the house**, *l'école* / **the school**, *les enfants* / **the children**

The definite articles are also used as direct object pronouns.

See **direct object pronoun** in this section. See also **definite articles** in §3.1.

Demonstrative adjective

A demonstrative adjective is an adjective that points something or someone out. It is placed in front of a noun.

Examples:
this book / *ce livre;* **this hotel** / *cet hôtel;* **this child** / *cet enfant;*
this house / *cette maison;* **these flowers** / *ces fleurs*

See **demonstrative adjectives** in §5.4–2.

Demonstrative pronoun

A demonstrative pronoun is a pronoun that points something
or someone out. It takes the place of a noun. It agrees in
gender and number with the noun it replaces.

Examples:
I have two apples; do you prefer this one or that one? / *J'ai deux
pommes; préférez-vous **celle-ci** ou **celle-là**?*
Sorry, but I prefer those. / *Je regrette, mais je préfère **celles-là**.*
Do you like the ones that are on the table? / *Aimez-vous **celles** qui
sont sur la table?*

For demonstrative pronouns that are neuter, see **neuter** in this
section.

Dependent clause

A dependent clause is a group of words that contains a
subject and a predicate. It does not express a complete
thought when it stands alone. It is called dependent because
it depends on the independent clause for a complete meaning.
Subordinate clause is another term for dependent clause.

Example:
Mary is absent today because she is sick. / *Marie est absente
aujourd'hui parce qu'elle est malade.* The independent clause is
Mary is absent today. The dependent clause is **because she
is sick**. Review *être* in the verb tables in §7.19. See also **clause**
and **independent clause** in this section.

Descriptive adjective

A descriptive adjective is an adjective that describes a person, place, or thing.

Examples:
a **pretty girl** / *une jolie jeune fille;* **a handsome boy** / *un beau garçon;* **a small house** / *une petite maison;* **a big city** / *une grande ville;* **an expensive car** / *une voiture chère*

Review descriptive adjectives in §5.4–1. See also **adjective** in this section.

Direct object noun

A direct object noun receives the action of the verb **directly**. That is why it is called a **direct object**, as opposed to an indirect object. A direct object noun is normally placed after the verb.

Examples:
I am writing a letter. / *J'écris une lettre.* The subject is **I** / *J' (Je).* The verb is **am writing** / *écris.* The direct object is the noun **letter** / *une lettre.*

I wrote a letter. / *J'ai écrit une lettre.* The subject is **I** / *J' (Je).* The verb is **wrote** / *ai écrit.* The direct object is the noun **letter** / *une lettre.*

See also **direct object pronoun** in this section.

Direct object pronoun

A direct object pronoun receives the action of the verb **directly**. It takes the place of a direct object noun. In French, a pronoun that is a direct object of a verb is ordinarily placed in front of the verb.

Example:
I am reading the letter. / *Je lis la lettre.*
I am reading it [the letter]. / *Je **la** lis.*

In the *passé composé*, the direct object pronoun precedes the helping verb. Although the verb is *avoir*, agreement is made on the past participle to match the gender and number of this *preceding* direct object pronoun.

> *J'ai lu la lettre.* / I read the letter.
> *Je l'ai lue.* / I read it.
> *Tu n'as pas lu les textos.* / You did not read the texts.
> *Tu ne les a pas lus.* / You did not read them.

See also **agreement of past participle with its preceding direct object** in this section.

A direct object pronoun is placed after the verb and joined with a hyphen in the affirmative imperative.

Example:
Write it [the letter] now. / *Écrivez-la maintenant.*

The direct object pronouns are summed up here:

Person	Singular		Plural	
1st	*me (m')* me		*nous*	us
2nd	*te (t')* you (familiar)		*vous*	you (singular polite or plural)
3rd	*le (l')* him, it (person or thing) *la (l')* her, it (person or thing)		*les*	them (persons or things)

See also **imperative** in this section. Consult the **imperative (command)** in §7.8–15 and **word order in a sentence** in §11.

Disjunctive pronoun

In French grammar, a disjunctive pronoun is a pronoun that is stressed; in other words, emphasis is placed on it.

Examples:

I speak well; he does not speak well. / *Moi, je parle bien; lui, il ne parle pas bien.*

Talk to me. / *Parlez-moi.*

A disjunctive pronoun is also an object of a preposition.

Examples:

She is talking with me. / *Elle parle avec moi.*

I always think of you. / *Je pense toujours à toi.*

The disjunctive pronouns are summed up here:

Person	Singular		Plural	
1st	*moi*	me	*nous*	us
2nd	*toi*	you (familiar)	*vous*	you (singular polite or plural)
3rd	*sol*	oneself		
	lui	him, he	*eux*	them, they (m.)
	elle	her, she	*elles*	them, they (f.)

Ending of a verb

In French grammar, the ending of a verb form changes according to the person and number of the subject and the tense of the verb.

Example:

To form the present indicative tense of a regular -*er* verb like parler, drop the -*er* ending of the infinitive and add the following endings: **-e, -es, -e** for the first, second, and third persons of the singular; **-ons, -ez, -ent** for the first, second, and third persons of the plural.

You then get:

je parle, tu parles, il (elle, on) parle
nous parlons, vous parlez, ils (elles) parlent

See also **stem of a verb** in this section.

§22

Feminine

In French grammar, the gender of a noun, pronoun, or adjective is feminine or masculine, not female or male.

Examples:

	Masculine	
noun	**pronoun**	**adjective**
le garçon	*il*	*grand*
the boy	he	tall
le livre	*il*	*petit*
the book	it	small

	Feminine	
noun	**pronoun**	**adjective**
la femme	*elle*	*grande*
the woman	she	tall
la voiture	*elle*	*petite*
the car	it	small

See also **gender** and **neuter** in this section.

Gender

In French and English grammar, gender means masculine or feminine.

Examples:
Masculine: **the boy** / *le garçon*; **he, it** / *il*; **the book** / *le livre*
Feminine: **the girl** / *la jeune fille*; **she, it** / *elle*; **the house** / *la maison*

Gerund

In English grammar, a gerund is a word formed from a verb. It ends in **ing**. Actually, it is the present participle of a verb, but it is not used as a verb; it is used as a noun.

Example:
Seeing is believing. / *Voir c'est croire.*

However, in French grammar, the infinitive form of the verb is used, as in the preceding example, when the verb is used as a noun. In French, **seeing is believing** is expressed as **to see is to believe**.

The French gerund is also a word formed from a verb. It ends in **ant**. It is also the present participle of a verb. As a gerund, it is normally preceded by the preposition *en*.

Example:
En partant, il a claqué la porte. / While leaving, he slammed the door.

See also **present participle** in this section.

Imperative

The imperative is a mood, not a tense. It is used to express a command. In French, it is used in the second person of the singular (*tu*), the second person of the plural (*vous*), and the first person of the plural (*nous*).

Examples:
Fais attention! / Be careful!
Fermez la porte, s'il vous plaît. / Close the door, please.
Mangeons! / Let's eat!

Review the **imperative (command)** with examples in §7.8–15. See also **mood of verbs** and **person (1st, 2nd, 3rd)** in this section.

Indefinite article

In English, the indefinite articles are **a** and **an**, as in **a book**, **an apple**. They are indefinite because they do not refer to any definite or particular noun.

In French there are two indefinite articles in the singular: one in the masculine form (*un*) and one in the feminine form (*une*).

> **Examples:**
> Masculine singular: *un livre* / **a book**
> Feminine singular: *une pomme* / **an apple**
>
> In French, they both change to *des* in the plural.

> **Examples:**
> I have a brother. / *J'ai un frère;* I have brothers. / *J'ai des frères.*
> I have a sister. / *J'ai une soeur;* I have sisters. / *J'ai des soeurs.*
> I have an apple. / *J'ai une pomme;* I have apples. / *J'ai des pommes.*

See also **definite article** in this section. Consult §3.1.

Indefinite pronoun

An indefinite pronoun is a pronoun that does not refer to any definite or particular noun.

> **Examples:**
> **something** / *quelque chose;* **someone, somebody** / *quelqu'un, quelqu'une;* **one, "they"** / *on* (3rd pers. sing.) as in *On ne sait jamais.* / One never knows; *On dit qu'il va neiger.* / They say it's going to snow; **each one** / *chacun, chacune;* **anything** / *n'importe quoi.*

Tip	Be careful when you use *on*, which can be understood as *nous* depending on the context. If there may be confusion, use a different indefinite pronoun such as *quelqu'un*.

On a brisé les vitres de la voiture de mon voisin.
Intended message: The windows of my neighbor's car were broken. OR One (Someone) broke the windows of my neighbor's car. Possible message: We (*Nous*) broke the windows of my neighbor's car. That is, you participated in the vandalism.

Instead, say something such as: *Quelqu'un a brisé les vitres de la voiture de mon voisin.* / Someone broke the windows of my neighbor's car.

Independent clause

An independent clause is a group of words that contains a subject and a predicate. It expresses a complete thought when it stands alone.

Example:
The cat is sleeping under the bed. / *Le chat dort sous le lit*.

See also **clause, dependent clause,** and **predicate** in this section.

Indicative mood

The indicative mood is used in sentences that make a statement or ask a question. The indicative mood is used most of the time when we speak or write in English or French.

Examples:
Where are you going? / *Où allez-vous?*
I am going home now. / *Je vais chez moi maintenant*.

See also **mood of verbs** in this section.

Indirect object noun

An indirect object noun receives the action of the verb *indirectly*.

> **Example:**
> I am writing a letter to Mary **or** I am writing Mary a letter. / *J'écris une lettre à Marie.*
> The subject is **I** / *Je*. The verb is **am writing** / *écris*. The direct object noun is **a letter** / *une lettre*. The indirect object noun is **to Mary** / *à Marie*. An agreement is not made with an indirect object noun.

See also **indirect object pronoun, direct object noun,** and **direct object pronoun** in this section.

Indirect object pronoun

An indirect object pronoun takes the place of an indirect object noun. It receives the action of the verb **indirectly**. In French a pronoun that is the indirect object of a verb is ordinarily placed in front of the verb.

> **Example:**
> I am writing a letter to her **or** I am writing her a letter. / *Je lui écris une lettre.* The indirect object pronoun is **(to) her** / *lui*.

An agreement is not made with an indirect object pronoun. An indirect object pronoun is placed after the verb and is joined with a hyphen in the affirmative imperative.

> **Example:**
> Write to her now. / *Écris-lui maintenant.*

The indirect object pronouns are summed up below:

Person	Singular		Plural	
1st	*me (m')*	to me	*nous*	to us
2nd	*te (t')*	to you (fam.)	*vous*	to you (singular polite or plural)
3rd	*lui*	to him, to her	*leur*	to them

Review the **imperative (command)** in §7.8–15. See also **indirect object noun** in this section.

Infinitive

An infinitive is a verb form. In English, it is normally stated with the preposition **to,** as in **to talk, to finish, to sell**. In French, the infinitive form of a verb consists of three major types: those of the first conjugation that end in *-er*, those of the second conjugation that end in *-ir*, and those of the third conjugation that end in *-re*.

Examples:
parler / **to talk, to speak;** *finir* / **to finish;** *vendre* / **to sell**

> **Tip** Verbs that end in *-oir (avoir, devoir, vouloir,* and others) can be considered a separate group. However, they do not follow a set pattern and must be learned individually.

Interjection

An interjection is a word that expresses emotion, a feeling of joy or sadness, an exclamation of surprise, and other exclamations consisting of one or two words.

Examples:
Ah! / *Ah!*
Oh! / *Oh!*
Darn it! / *Zut!*
Whew! / *Ouf!*

Interrogative adjective

An interrogative adjective is an adjective used in a question. It agrees in gender and number with the noun it modifies.

Examples:
What book do you want? / *Quel livre désirez-vous?*
What time is it? / *Quelle heure est-il?*

See also §5.4–3.

Interrogative adverb

An interrogative adverb is an adverb that introduces a question. As an adverb, it modifies the verb.

Examples:
How are you? / *Comment allez-vous?*
How much does this book cost? / *Combien coûte ce livre?*
When are you leaving? / *Quand partez-vous?*

See also §8.3–1.

Interrogative pronoun

An interrogative pronoun is a pronoun that asks a question. There are interrogative pronouns that refer to persons and those that refer to things.

Examples:
Who is on the phone? / *Qui est à l'appareil?*
What are you saying? / *Que dites-vous?* or *Qu'est-ce que vous dites?*

See also §6.1–10.

Interrogative sentence

An interrogative sentence asks a question.

Example:
What are you doing? / *Que faites-vous?* (inversion) or *Qu'est-ce que vous faites?* (with *qu'est-ce que*)

See also declarative sentence in this section.

Intransitive verb

An intransitive verb is a verb that does not take a direct object.

Example:
The professor is talking too fast. / *Le professeur parle trop rapidement.*

An intransitive verb takes an indirect object.

Example:
The professor is talking to us. / *Le professeur nous parle.*

See also **direct object noun, direct object pronoun, indirect object pronoun**, and **transitive verb** in this section.

Irregular verb

An irregular verb is a verb that does not follow a fixed pattern in its conjugation in the various verb tenses.

Examples of basic irregular verbs in French:
aller / **to go**
avoir / **to have**
être / **to be**
faire / **to do, to make**

Review irregular verbs in the present indicative tense and the imperative (command). See also **conjugation** and **regular verb** in this section.

Limiting adjective

A limiting adjective is an adjective that limits a quantity.

> **Example:**
> **three tickets** / *trois billets*

Main clause

Main clause is another term for independent clause.

See **independent clause** in this section.

Masculine

In French grammar, the gender of a noun, pronoun, or adjective is masculine or feminine, not male or female. See also **feminine, gender**, and **neuter** in this section.

Mood of verbs

Some grammarians use the term **the mode** instead of **the mood** of a verb. Either term means the manner or *way* in which a verb is expressed. In English and French grammar, a verb expresses an action or state of being in the following three moods (modes, *ways*): the indicative mood, the imperative mood, and the subjunctive mood. In French grammar, there is also the infinitive mood when the whole infinitive is used; for example *voir* and *croire*, as in *Voir c'est croire* / Seeing is believing (literally, to see is to believe). Most of the time in English and French, we speak and write in the indicative mood.

See also **indicative mood** in this section.

Negative statement, affirmative statement

See **affirmative statement, negative statement** in this section.

Neuter

A word that is neuter is neither masculine nor feminine. Common neuter demonstrative pronouns are *ce (c')* / **it**, *ceci* / **this**, *cela* / **that**, *ça* / **that**. They are invariable, which means they do not change in gender and number. When you use one of these neuter demonstrative pronouns, you should make a masculine agreement. For example, even if you are talking about pizza (*la pizza*), you say *C'est bon!* because of the neuter *ce (c')*. However, you make the agreement when you say *Elle est bonne!* / It is good! In this sentence, the pronoun *elle* agrees in gender and number with *la pizza*.

Examples:
It's not true / *Ce n'est pas vrai;* it is true / *c'est vrai;* this is true / *ceci est vrai;* that is true / *cela est vrai;* what is that? / *qu'est-ce que c'est que ça?*

There is also the neuter pronoun *le*, as in *Je le pense* / I think so.

For demonstrative pronouns that are not neuter, see **demonstrative pronoun** in this section. See also **feminine** and **gender**.

Noun

A noun is a word that names a person, animal, place, thing, condition or state, or quality.

Examples:
the man / *l'homme,* **the woman** / *la femme,* **the horse** / *le cheval,* **the house** / *la maison,* **the book** / *le livre,* **happiness** / *le bonheur,* **excellence** / *l'excellence* (fem.)

In French, the noun *le nom* is the word for **name** (*Quel est votre nom?* / What is your name?) and also for **noun** (*Un adjectif sert à qualifier un nom.* / An adjective is used to qualify a noun.)

Number

In English and French grammar, number means singular or plural.

> **Examples:**
> Masc. sing.: **the boy** / *le garçon;* **the arm** / *le bras;* **the eye** / *l'oeil*
> Masc. pl.: **the boys** / *les garçons;* **the arms** / *les bras;* **the eyes** / *les yeux*
> Fem. sing.: **the girl** / *la jeune fille;* **the house** / *la maison;* **the hen** / *la poule*
> Fem. pl.: **the girls** / *les jeunes filles;* **the houses** / *les maisons;* **the hens** / *les poules*

Ordinal number

An ordinal number expresses position in a series, such as **first, second, third,** and so on. In English and French grammar, we talk about first person, second person, third person singular or plural regarding subjects and verbs. Review the ordinal numbers and consult the Index. See also **cardinal number** and **person (1st, 2nd, 3rd)** in this section.

Tip	Ordinal numbers are used to describe an order in a sequence. "Tom was tired because he'd taken his fiftieth order of the day."

Orthographical changes in verb forms

An orthographical change in a verb form is a change in spelling.

> **Examples:**
> The second letter *c* in the verb *commencer* / **to begin** changes to *ç* if the letter after it is *a, o,* or *u,* as in *nous commençons* / **we begin**. The reason for this spelling change is to preserve the sound of *s* as it is pronounced in the infinitive form *commencer*.
> Ordinarily, when *a, o,* or *u* follow the letter *c,* the *c* is pronounced as in the sound of *k*. The mark under the letter *ç* is called *une*

cédille / a cedilla. Some linguists say it is the lower part of the letter *s* and it tells you to pronounce *ç* as an *s* sound. Other linguists say that the letter *ç* was borrowed from the Greek alphabet's *sigma* (*ç*), which represents the sound of *s*.

The verb *s'appeler* / **to call oneself, to be named** contains a single *l*. When a verb form is stressed on the syllable containing one *l*, it doubles, as in *je m'appelle...* / **I call myself . . . , my name is . . . .**

Review orthographically changing verbs in §7.17.

Partitive

In French grammar, the partitive denotes a *part* of a whole. In English, we express the partitive by saying **some** or **any** in front of the noun. In French, we use the following partitive forms in front of the noun:

Masculine singular: *du* or *de l'*
Feminine singular: *de la* or *de l'*
Masculine or feminine plural: *des*
(Note : The plural is rare in the partitive because the partitive is not used for countable things: *des pâtes* / **some pasta;** *des épinards* / **some spinach.** When you use *des* with countable things, you are not using the partitive. You are using the plural indefinite article: *un ami* (a friend) / *des amis* (friends); *une carotte* (a carrot) / *des carottes* (carrots); *un stylo* (a pen) / *des stylos* (pens). See §3.2.)

Examples:

I have some coffee. / *J'ai du café.*
Bring me some water, please. / *Apportez-moi de l'eau, s'il vous plaît.*
Is there any meat? / *Y a-t-il de la viande?*
Do you have any pasta? / *Avez-vous des pâtes?*

In the negative, these partitive forms change to *de* or *d'*:

I don't have any coffee. / *Je n'ai pas de café.*
I don't want any water. / *Je ne veux pas d'eau.*
There isn't any meat. / *Il n'y a pas de viande.*
No, I don't have any pasta. / *Non, je n'ai pas de pâtes.*

Review the partitive in §3.3.

Passé composé

The *passé composé* is a commonly used past tense. It is composed of two parts, an auxiliary verb (also called a helping verb: *avoir* or *être*) conjugated in the present tense, along with a past participle.

Example:
Madeleine est allée au cinéma avec ses amis. / Madeleine went to the movies with her friends.

See also **auxiliary verb** and **past participle** in this section. Also consult §7.8–8.

Passive voice

When we speak or write in the active voice and change to the passive voice, the direct object becomes the subject, the subject becomes the object of a preposition, and the verb becomes **to be** plus the past participle of the active verb. The past participle functions as an adjective.

Example:
Janine is loved by everyone. / *Janine est aimée de tout le monde.* The subject is **Janine**. The verb is **is** / *est*. The object of the preposition **by** / *de* is **everyone** / *tout le monde*. Compare the preceding sentence with the example *(Tout le monde aime Janine.)* in the **active voice** in this section.

Past indefinite tense

In French, this tense is the *passé composé*. See *passé composé* in this section and review §7.8–8.

Past participle

A past participle is derived from a verb. It is used to form the compound tenses, such as the *passé composé*. Its auxiliary verb in English is **to have**. In French, the auxiliary verb is *avoir* / **to have** or *être* / **to be**. The auxiliary is part of the verb tense.

Examples with *avoir* as the auxiliary verb:
Elle a mangé. / **She has eaten.** (She ate; she did eat.) The
subject is *elle* / **she**. The verb is *a mangé* / **has eaten**. The tense
of the verb is the *passé composé*. The auxiliary verb is *a* / **has**.
The past participle is *mangé* / **eaten**.

Examples with *être* as the auxiliary verb:
Elle est arrivée. / **She has arrived.** (She arrived; she did arrive.)
The verb is *est arrivée* / **has arrived**. The tense of the verb is the
passé composé. The auxiliary verb is *est* / **has**. The past participle is *arrivée* / **arrived**.

See §7.1 and §7.2.

Person (1st, 2nd, 3rd)

Verb forms in a particular tense are learned systematically
according to person (1st, 2nd, 3rd) and number (singular,
plural).
The following example shows the present indicative tense of
the verb *aller* / **to go:**

Singular		Plural	
1st person:	*je vais*	1st person:	*nous allons*
2nd person:	*tu vas*	2nd person:	*vous allez*
3rd person:	*il, elle va*	3rd person:	*ils, elles vont*

Personal pronoun

A personal pronoun refers to a person. Review the subject
pronouns in §6.1–1. For examples of other types of pronouns,
see also **demonstrative pronoun, direct object pronoun,
disjunctive pronoun, indefinite pronoun, indirect object
pronoun, interrogative pronoun, reflexive pronoun, and
relative pronoun** in this section.

§22

Plural

Plural means more than one. See also **person (1st, 2nd, 3rd)** and **singular** in this section.

Possessive adjective

A possessive adjective is an adjective that is placed in front of a noun to show possession. In French, their forms change in gender (masculine or feminine) and number (singular or plural) to agree with the noun they modify.

> **Examples:**
> **my book** / *mon livre*   **my car** / *ma voiture*
> **my books** / *mes livres*   **my cars** / *mes voitures*

Predicate

The predicate is the part of the sentence that tells us something about the subject. The main word of the predicate is the verb.

> **Example:**
> The tourists are waiting for the tour bus. / *Les touristes attendent l'autocar.*
>
> The subject is **the tourists** / *les touristes.* The predicate is **are waiting for the tour bus** / *attendent l'autocar.* The verb is **are waiting** / *attendent.* The direct object is **the tour bus** / *l'autocar.*

Preposition

A preposition is a word that establishes a rapport between words.

> **Examples (with, in, on, at, between):**
> **with** me / *avec moi*
> **in** the drawer / *dans le tiroir*
> **on** the table / *sur la table*
> **at** six o'clock / *à six heures*
> **between** him and her / *entre lui et elle*

Present indicative tense

This is a commonly used tense. It is defined with examples in French and English in §7.8–1.

Present participle

A present participle is derived from a verb form. In French it is regularly formed like this: Take the *nous* form of the present indicative tense of the verb you have in mind, then drop the ending *ons* and add *ant*. In English, a present participle ends in **ing**.

Examples:

Infinitive	Present Indicative nous form	Present participle
chanter	*nous chantons*	*chantant*
to sing	we sing	singing
finir	*nous finissons*	*finissant*
to finish	we finish	finishing
vendre	*nous vendons*	*vendant*
to sell	we sell	selling

Pronoun

A pronoun is a word that takes the place of a noun.

Examples:
l'homme / **il**   *l'arbre* / **il**
the man / **he**   the tree / **it**
la femme / **elle**   *la voiture* / **elle**
the woman / **she**   the car / **it**

For examples of other kinds of pronouns, see also **demonstrative pronoun**, **direct object pronoun**, **disjunctive pronoun**, **indefinite pronoun**, **indirect object pronoun**, **interrogative pronoun**, **reflexive pronoun**, and **relative pronoun** in this section.

§22

Reflexive pronoun and reflexive verb

In English, a reflexive pronoun is a personal pronoun that contains **-self** or **-selves**. In French and English, a reflexive pronoun is used with a verb that is called reflexive because the action of the verb falls (is reflected back) on the reflexive pronoun. In French, as in English, there is a required set of reflexive pronouns for a reflexive verb.

> **Examples:**
> *se laver* / to wash oneself
> *Je me lave.* / I wash myself.
> *se blesser* / to hurt oneself
> *Elle s'est blessée.* / She hurt herself.

In French, a reflexive verb is conjugated with *être* to form a compound tense. The French term for a reflexive verb is *un verbe pronominal* because a pronoun goes with the verb. See also **agreement of past participle of a reflexive verb with its reflexive pronoun** in this section.

Regular verb

A regular verb is a verb that is conjugated in the various tenses according to a fixed pattern. For examples, review regular *-er*, *-ir*, and *-re* verbs in the present indicative tense. Consult the Index. See also **conjugation** and **irregular verb** in this section.

Relative pronoun

A relative pronoun is a pronoun that refers to its antecedent.

> **Example:**
> The woman who won the award is my mother. / *La femme qui a gagné le prix est ma mère.* The antecedent is **woman** / *la femme*. The relative pronoun **who** / *qui* refers to the woman.

See also **antecedent** in this section. See §6.1–13.

Sentence

A sentence is a group of words that contains a subject and a predicate. The verb is contained in the predicate. A sentence expresses a complete thought.

> **Example:**
> The train leaves from the North Station at two o'clock in the afternoon. / *Le train part de la Gare du Nord à deux heures de l'après-midi.* The subject is **train** / *le train*. The predicate is **leaves from the North Station at two o'clock in the afternoon** / *part de la Gare du Nord à deux heures de l'après-midi.* The verb is **leaves** / *part*.

See also **complex sentence, compound sentence, and simple sentence** in this section.

Simple sentence

A simple sentence is a sentence that contains one subject and one predicate. The verb is the core of the predicate. The verb is the most important word in a sentence because it tells us what the subject is doing.

> **Example:**
> Mary is eating an apple from her garden. / *Marie mange une pomme de son jardin.* The subject is **Mary** / *Marie*. The predicate is **is eating** / *mange*. The direct object is **an apple** / *une pomme*. **From her garden** / *de son jardin* is an adverbial phrase. It tells you where the apple came from.

See also **complex sentence** and **compound sentence** in this section.

Singular

Singular means one. See also **person (1st, 2nd, 3rd)** and **plural** in this section.

Spelling changes in verb forms

See **orthographical changes in verb forms** in this section.

Stem of a verb

The stem of a verb is what is left after we drop the ending of its infinitive form. It is added to the required endings of a regular verb in a particular verb tense.

Examples:

Infinitive	Ending of infinitive	Stem
donner / to give	*er*	*donn*
choisir / to choose	*ir*	*chois*
vendre / to sell	*re*	*vend*

See also **ending of a verb** in this section.

Subject

A subject is the part of a sentence that is related to its verb. The verb says something about the subject.

Examples:
Mary and Catherine are beautiful. / *Marie et Catherine sont belles.*
Peter and Paul are handsome. / *Pierre et Paul sont beaux.*

Subjunctive mood

The subjunctive mood of a verb is used in specific cases; for example, it is used after certain verbs expressing a wish, doubt, emotion, fear, joy, uncertainty, an indefinite expression, an indefinite antecedent, certain conjunctions, and others. Review the present subjunctive mood of *avoir* and *être* in §7.19. See also **mood of verbs** in this section.

Subordinate clause

Subordinate clause is another term for dependent clause. See also **dependent clause** in this section.

Superlative adjective

A superlative adjective is an adjective that expresses the highest degree when making a comparison of more than two persons or things.

Examples:

	Adjective	Comparative	Superlative
(masc.)	*bon* / good	*meilleur* / better	*le meilleur* / (the) best
(fem.)	*bonne* / good	*meilleure* / better	*la meilleure* / (the) best
(masc.)	*mauvais* / bad	*plus mauvais* / worse	*le plus mauvais* / (the) worst
(fem.)	*mauvaise* / bad	*plus mauvaise* / worse	*la plus mauvaise* / (the) worst

See also **comparative adjective** in this list. See §5.4–6.

Superlative adverb

A superlative adverb is an adverb that expresses the highest degree when making a comparison of more than two persons or things.

Example:

Adverb	Comparative	Superlative
vite / quickly	*plus vite* / more quickly	*le plus vite* / most quickly
	moins vite / less quickly	*le moins vite* / least quickly

See §8.3–3.

§22

Tense of verb

In English and French grammar, tense means time. The tense of the verb indicates the time of the action or state of being. The three major segments of time are past, present, and future. Review the verb tables in §7.19.

Transitive verb

A transitive verb is a verb that takes a direct object.

> **Example:**
> I am closing the window. / *Je ferme la fenêtre.* The subject is **I** / *Je.* The verb is **am closing** / *ferme.* The direct object is **the window** / *la fenêtre.* The action of the verb is carried out on the direct object.

See also **intransitive** in this section.

Verb

A verb is a word that expresses action or a state of being.

> **Example of action:**
> *Nous sommes allées au cinéma hier soir.* / We went to the movies last night.
> The verb is *sommes allés* / **went**.

> **Example of state of being:**
> *La jeune fille est heureuse.* / The girl is happy.
> The verb is *est* / **is**.

Review *aller* and *être* in §7.19.

French-English Vocabulary

à *prep.* at, to
à moins que *conj.* unless
actif, active *adj.* active
aéroport *n.m.* airport
affreusement *adv.* frightfully
ai *v. form of* avoir
aimable *adj.* amiable, likeable, pleasant, kind
aimer *v.* to love; aimer bien to like
Allemagne *n.f.* Germany
allemand *n.m.* German (language); Allemand, Allemande *n.* German (person)
aller *v.* to go; s'en aller to go away
allez-vous-en! go away!
allons! let's go!
amèrement *adv.* bitterly
ami, amie *n.* friend
amour *n.m.* love
amusant, amusante *adj.* funny, amusing
an *n.m.* year
ancien, ancienne *adj.* old, ancient
anglais *n.m.* English (language); Anglais, Anglaise *n.* English (person)
Angleterre *n.f.* England
appeler *v.* to call; s'appeler *reflexive v.* to call oneself, to be named
après *prep.*, *adv.* after; après-midi *n.m.* afternoon
arbre *n.m.* tree
argent *n.m.* money
Asie *n.f.* Asia
asseoir *v.* to seat; s'asseoir *reflexive v.* to sit down; asseyez-vous! sit down!

assez (de) *adv.* enough (of); assez bien quite well, well enough
assieds-toi! sit down!
au to the, at the; contraction of à + le
aujourd'hui *adv.* today
aussi *adv.* also, too
aussi . . . que *conj.* as . . . as
Australie *n.f.* Australia
auteur *n.m.*, auteure *n.f.* author
autre *adj.* other; *pron.* another
autrefois *adv.* formerly
aux to the, at the; contraction of à + les
avec *prep.* with
avez *v. form of* avoir
avocat *n.m.* lawyer; une avocate woman lawyer
avoir *v.* to have

bas *n.m.* stocking; *adv.* low; en bas down, downstairs; *adj.* bas, basse low
beau *adj. m.* handsome, beautiful
beaucoup (de) *adv.* many, much (of)
bel *adj. m.* handsome, beautiful (Use bel before a vowel or mute *h*: un bel hôtel / a beautiful hotel)
belle *adj. f.* beautiful, handsome
bénir *v.* to bless
besoin *n.m.* need; avoir besoin de to need, to have need of
bibliothèque *n.f.* library
bien *adv.* well
bientôt *adv.* soon
billet *n.m.* ticket, note
blanc, blanche *adj.* white

adj.: adjective; adv.: adverb; conj.: conjunction; f.: feminine; m.: masculine; n.: noun; pl.: plural; prep.: preposition; pron.: pronoun; sing.: singular; v.: verb

blesser *v.* to injure, to wound
boire *v.* to drink
bon, bonne *adj.* good
bonbons *n.m.* candies
bouche *n.f.* mouth (of a person); **la gueule** (mouth of an animal)
but *n.m.* goal

ça *pron.* shortening of **cela**
cadeau *n.m.* gift, present
café *n.m.* coffee
cahier *n.m.* notebook
campagne *n.f.* country(side)
catholique *n.m.f.* Catholic
ce *demons. adj.* this; **ce stylo** this pen; **ce livre** this book; **ce garçon** this boy
cela *pron.* that; **Aimez-vous cela?** Do you like that?
chanter *v.* to sing
chanteur, chanteuse *n.m.f.* singer
chapeau *n.m.* hat
chaque *adj.* each
chaud, chaude *adj.* warm, hot
chaussette *n.f.* sock
chaussure *n.f.* shoe
chef *n.m.* chief, boss, chef
cheveu, cheveux *n.m.* hair
chez *prep.* at the place of, at the home of, at the shop of; **chez moi** at my place
choisir *v.* to choose, to select
chose *n.f.* thing; **quelque chose** something
cinéma *n.m.* movies (theater)
clé, clef *n.f.* key
coin *n.m.* corner
combien (de) *adv.* how much (of), how many (of)
comprendre *v.* to understand
copain *n.m.*, **copine** *n.f.* pal, buddy
cravate *n.f.* necktie
crayon *n.m.* pencil
croire *v.* to believe
cruel, cruelle *adj.* cruel

dame *n.f.* lady
dans *prep.* in
de *prep.* of, from
dehors *adv.* outside
déjà *adv.* already; **déjà vu** already seen
dent *n.f.* tooth
depuis *adv.* since; **depuis longtemps** for a long time
dernier, dernière *adj.* last
des of the, from the; contraction of **de + les**; some
dimanche *n.m.* Sunday
dire *v.* to say, to tell; **vouloir dire** to mean
donc *conj.* therefore, consequently
donner *v.* to give
dont *pron.* of which, whose
dormir *v.* to sleep
douche *n.f.* shower (bath)
douter *v.* to doubt
drôle *adj.* funny, droll
du of the, from the; contraction of **de + le**; some
dû *past participle of* **devoir**; ought to, must

eau *n.f.* water
école *n.f.* school; **à l'école** in (at, to) school; **une école de danse** dance school
écouter *v.* to listen (to)
écrire *v.* to write
écrivons *v. form of* **écrire**
égal, égaux, égale, égales *adj.* equal
église *n.f.* church
en *pron.* of it, of them, some of it, some of them; *prep.* in
encore *adv.* still, yet, again
encre *n.f.* ink
enregistrer *v.* to record (on a tape, record)
enseigner *v.* to teach
entendre *v.* to hear, to understand
enthousiasme *n.m.* enthusiasm

entre *prep.* between; *also a v. form of* **entrer (dans)** to enter (into)
envers *prep.* toward
environ *adv.* nearly, about
envoyer *v.* to send; **envoyer chercher** to send for
Espagne *n.f.* Spain
espagnol *n.m.* Spanish (language); **Espagnol, Espagnole** *n.* Spanish (person)
est *present indicative of* **être**
Etats-Unis *n.m.pl.* United States
été *n.m.* summer; *also past participle of* **être**
être *v.* to be
étudiant, étudiante *n.m.* student
étudier *v.* to study
eu *past participle of* **avoir**

faim *n.f.* hunger; **avoir faim** to be hungry
faire *v.* to do, to make; **faire un voyage** to take a trip
falloir *v.* to be necessary; **il faut** it is necessary
faux, fausse *adj.* false
favori, favorite *adj.* favorite
femme *n.f.* woman; *when possessive, wife;* **ma femme** my wife
fête *n.f.* feast, holiday, party
feu *n.m.* fire; **le feu rouge** red light (traffic)
février *n.m.* February
fille *n.f.* daughter; **la jeune fille** girl
fils *n.m.* son
finir *v.* to finish, to end
forêt *n.f.* forest
fourchette *n.f.* fork
français *n.m.* French (language); **Français, Française** *n.* French (person)
franchement *adv.* frankly
frère *n.m.* brother
fromage *n.m.* cheese
fuir *v.* to flee, to run away; *past participle* **fui**

garçon *n.m.* boy
gâteau *n.m.* cake
gentil, gentille *adj.* nice, pleasant
gentiment *adv.* gently
gomme *n.f.* eraser (rubber)
grand, grande *adj.* great, big, large; **un grand magasin** department store
Grande Bretagne *n.f.* Great Britain
gris, grise *adj.* gray
gros, grosse *adj.* big, fat, large

heureusement *adv.* fortunately, happily
heureux, heureuse *adj.* happy
homme *n.m.* man
honneur *n.m.* honor
huître *n.f.* oyster

ici *adv.* here
île *n.f.* isle, island
immeuble *n.m.* (apartment) building
interrompre *v.* to interrupt
italien *n.m.* Italian (language); **Italien, Italienne** *n.* Italian (person)

janvier *n.m.* January
jeune *adj.* young
jeune fille *n.f.* girl
joli, jolie *adj.* pretty
jouer *v.* to play
jouet *n.m.* toy
jour *n.m.* day
journal *n.m.* newspaper
journée *n.f.* (all) day (long)

la *definite article, f.* the; *also direct object pronoun, f. sing.* it, her
laid, laide *adj.* ugly
laideur *n.f.* ugliness
laver *v.* to wash (something or someone); **se laver** *reflex. verb* to wash oneself
le *definite article, m.* the; *also direct object pronoun, m. sing.* it, him
lent, lente *adj.* slow

lentement *adv.* slowly
les *definite article, m. and f.* the; *also direct object pronoun, m. and f., pl.* them (people or things)
leur *possessive adj.* their; *also indirect object pron.* to them
lire *v.* to read; *past participle* **lu**
lit *n.m.* bed; *also present indicative, 3rd person sing. of* **lire**
livre *n.m.* book; **la livre** pound
Londres *n.m.* London
long, longue *adj.* long
longtemps *adv.* long time; **depuis longtemps** since a long time, for a long time
lorsque *adv.* when; *synonym of* **quand**
lui *indirect object pron., 3rd person sing.* to him, to her
lundi *n.m.* Monday

ma *possessive adj., f. sing.* my; **ma maison** my house
magasin *n.m.* store; **un grand magasin** department store
magazine *n.m.* magazine
maintenant *adv.* now
mais *conj.* but
maison *n.f.* house
malheur *n.m.* unhappiness
malheureusement *n.f.* unfortunately
manger *v.* to eat
marcher *v.* to walk, to march, to run (a machine)
mardi *n.m.* Tuesday
mars *n.m.* March
matin *n.m.* morning; **le matin** in the morning
médecin *n.m.* doctor
médecine *n.f.* medicine (profession)
médicament *n.m.* medicine (that you take)
meilleur, meilleure *adj.* better
mer *n.f.* sea
mère *n.f.* mother
mettre *v.* to put, to place; to put on (clothing)

mieux *adv.* better
monnaie *n.f.* change (money); coins
monsieur *n.m.* gentleman, sir, Mr.
mourir *v.* to die

naître *v.* to be born; *past participle* **né**
natation *n.f.* swimming
noir, noire *adj.* black
nom *n.m.* name
nouveau, nouvel, nouvelle *adj.* new

œil *n.m.* eye; **les yeux** eyes
œuf *n.m.* egg
oiseau *n.m.* bird
on *personal pron., 3rd person sing.* one (they)
oser *v.* to dare
ou *conj.* or; **où** *adv.* where
ouvrir *v.* to open; *past participle* **ouvert**

pain *n.m.* bread
papier *n.m.* paper
par *prep.* by; **par terre** on the floor, on the ground
parapluie *n.m.* umbrella
parc *n.m.* park
paresse *n.f.* laziness
paresseux, paresseuse *adj.* lazy
parler *v.* to talk, to speak
partir *v.* to leave; *past participle* **parti**
passer *v.* to spend (time); to go by, to pass by, to pass
pendant *prep.* during; **pendant que** *conj.* while
perdre *v.* to lose; *past participle* **perdu(e)(s)**
père *n.m.* father
perspicacité *n.f.* perspicacity, insight
peu (de) *adv.* little (of)
peur *n.f.* fear; **avoir peur** to be afraid, to feel afraid
peut *present indicative of* **pouvoir**

pied *n.m.* foot; **aller à pied** to walk

plage *n.f.* beach, seashore

pleuvoir *v.* to rain; *past participle* **plu**

plus *adv.* more; **plus de, plus que** more than

plusieurs *adv.* several

poule *n.f.* hen

poupée *n.f.* doll

pousser *v.* to push, to bud (flowers)

pouvoir *v.* to be able, can

précise *adj.* precise, precisely

prendre *v.* to take

presse *n.f.* press (printing)

public, publique *adj.* public

puis *adv.* then

quand *adv.* when; *synonym of* **lorsque**

quel, quelle, quels, quelles *adj.* which, what

quelque(s) *adj.* some; **quelque chose** something

quelquefois *adv.* sometimes

qui *pron.* who, whom

qui est-ce qui *pron.* who

quitter *v.* to leave (a person or place)

quoi *pron.* what (as obj. of a prep.); **avec quoi** with what

rang *n.m.* rank, row

restaurant *n.m.* restaurant

rire *v.* to laugh; *n.m.* laughter

robe *n.f.* dress

rose *n.f.* rose; *adj.* pink

rue *n.f.* street

samedi *n.m.* Saturday

sans *prep.* without

se *reflexive pron.* himself, herself, oneself

sec, sèche *adj.* dry

seize sixteen

semaine *n.f.* week

si *conj.* if

sœur *n.f.* sister

soir *n.m.* evening; **le soir** in the evening

son *n.m.* sound; *possessive adj.* his, her, its

sont *v.* form of **être**

sous *prep.* under

souvent *adv.* often

stylo *n.m.* pen

sucette *n.f.* lollipop; **sucer** *v.* to suck

sur *prep.* on

tenir *v.* to hold

thé *n.m.* tea

très *adv.* very

trop (de) *adv.* too much (of), too many (of)

trouver *v.* to find; **se trouver** *reflexive v.* to be located

tuer *v.* to kill

un *indefinite article, m. sing.* a, an (one); *fem.,* **une**

vacances *n.f.pl.* vacation; **les grandes vacances** summer vacation

vache *n.f.* cow

vais *present indicative of* **aller**

vendre *v.* to sell

venir *v.* to come

vent *n.m.* wind; **il fait du vent** it's windy

viande *n.f.* meat

vient *present indicative of* **venir**

vieux, vieil, vieille *adj.* old

vin *n.m.* wine

vingt twenty

voir *v.* to see; *past participle* **vu**

voyage *n.m.* trip; **faire un voyage** to take a trip, go on a trip; **Bon voyage!** Have a good trip!

y *adverbial pron.* there, in it, on it

yeux *n.m.* eyes; **l'œil** the eye

zèbre *n.m.* zebra

Index

Numbers refer to sections designated by the symbol § in this book.